MEMORIES of the LAND

PLACENAMES
OF
SAN LUIS OBISPO COUNTY

by
Mark P. Hall-Patton

EZ Nature Books
San Luis Obispo, California

"Names are part of the historic fabric of our lives, woven through our countryside, marking history and features of mountains and towns, creeks and valleys."

ISBN 0-945092-36-9
COPYRIGHT   1994 Mark P. Hall-Patton

Publisher: EZ Nature Books
P.O. Box 4206
San Luis Obispo, CA 93403

Distribution: Central Coast Books
P.O. Box 3654
San Luis Obispo, CA 93403

Cover photograph by Joseph A. Dickerson

Except as otherwise noted, all photos courtesy of San Luis Obispo County Historical Museum

Introduction

"Once, from eastern ocean to western ocean, the land stretched away without names. Nameless headlands split the surf; nameless lakes reflected nameless mountains; nameless rivers flowed through nameless valleys into nameless bays."

George Stewart, <u>Names on the Land</u>

No longer is the land without names. Names are part of the historic fabric of our lives, woven through our countryside, marking history and features of mountains and towns, creeks and valleys. They help us to define our place on the land, and to commemorate our lives and actions.

I think we all share an interest in what a name means, and where it comes from. We have all asked the who, what, and where questions regarding the names of places where we are, wondering about those who came before us, and left their names for us to find and wonder about.

Our earliest placenames date from long before the coming of the Spanish to our county. The Chumash and Salinan Indians, residents of San Luis Obispo County for many thousands of years, have left their names on the land today in places like Pismo Beach and Cholame, Huasna and Nipomo. This is part of their legacy to us, their not always so grateful successors.

Placenames also commemorate events which are long past, such as two sites in our county called "The Battleground." In both cases they relate to long ago fights in which people died fighting over concerns which are no longer part of our lives. In cases such as these, we can learn, hopefully, from our past.

In other cases, the names are applied because of natural features, such as Bee Rock or Chimney Rock. Though the original feature may not still exist, the names continue. The bee hive in Bee Rock, for example, was burned out many years ago, but the name remains to commemorate this partially forgotten phenomenon.

Still other prosaic names are taken from the presence of certain colors, such as Black Mountain or Red Rock, or other descriptions of the countryside, such as Rocky Canyon or Long Ridge. In these cases, the names are not of great historical interest, though one must be careful. White Point on Morro Bay, where the Morro Bay State Museum of Natural History is located, is not named for its color, but rather for Frederick White, a County Supervisor who owned the land.

Some of the most interesting place names, though, are those which refer to people. Grover Beach, Keyes Canyon, Huff's Hole Creek, or Garrity Peak are such examples in our county. In some cases the people are well remembered, in many cases they are not. Huff's Hole Creek, for example, commemo- rates a sheepherder who happened to camp on the creek. It is probably the only memory of this individual we have, but it is still with us.

One of the first questions I remember receiving at the San Luis Obispo County Historical Museum was the origin of the name of Freeborn Mountain. At the time I did not know, and there was no easy reference to which I could turn. I began to gather information from many sources into files on placenames in the county, inadvertently beginning to work on this book.

As with any book of this nature, the work is not the

author's alone. I have gathered from many people's work, picking out information from here and there. Many local history books have references to a few placenames, but these are seldom easily found. This book is intended to bring together the work of these other historians, as well as my own.

Other local historians have preceded me in working to document local placenames. A little remembered first work was published in 1916 by the Holmes Book Company. Written by H. M. Moreno, who noted with pride his residence in San Luis Obispo on the titlepage of the work, it was a good introduction to statewide placenames. Some of his explanations of local placenames, most notably that of Nacimiento, are of interest today.

After Moreno's work, the next work I am aware of relating to specifically local names was written by a predecessor of mine at the San Luis Obispo County Historical Museum, Louisiana Clayton Dart. Her short work entitled <u>What's In A Name?</u> is still the starting place for placename researchers today.

While noting other placename works, the articles by Dr. Appleton and Kathryn Klar in the Occasional Papers of the San Luis Obispo County Archaeological Society on Chumash Place Names in John Peabody Harrington's notes are invaluable resources for the impact of our earliest inhabitants on today's names. They are well worth having in any local placenames library.

I would like to acknowledge, with thanks, a few other specific individuals who had a great impact on this work. First and foremost, a man who had no idea that his work would inspire this imitator. This was Don Meadows, the dean of Orange County, California historians, and an old friend of my family. I have used his <u>Historic Placenames in Orange County</u>

for many years, and was inspired with a love of the romance of placenames from his work.

Closer to home, I want to acknowledge Dr. Dan Krieger, a friend and fellow toiler in the trenches. Dan's involvement with local history in San Luis Obispo County is too well known to need reiterating. However, it was he who first pushed me into local history writing, and began the course towards completion of this work. Dan also reviewed the manuscript, for which I thank him.

Three other local historians reviewed the final product. These were Harold Miossi, Al Davis, and Gordon Bennett. These three put in much effort in reading, annotating and correcting the manuscript. In each case they brought a long interest and fair judgement to the review effort. I am in their debt for all their time and efforts. However, it must always be said that any errors are mine alone.

Many others have helped with the final product. I want to especially thank the late Lura Rawson, my predecessor as Director of the San Luis Obispo County Historical Museum, Fraser MacGillivrey, Taylor Coffman, Lisa Kok of the Boundaries and Names Unit of the Geological Survey, Pat Nicholson, Dick Miller, Jim Norris, Ed Zolkoski, the Docents of the County Historical Museum, and so many others who offered their knowledge, suggestions and support. All contributed materially to this listing. A special thank you is also due Bill Charlesworth, for making possible the publication of the final product.

If, upon reading this book, you question a meaning or know the meaning of a placename not listed, feel free to contact me. There were names I was not able to find, names where I have hazarded a supposition based on other research, and others which I may never have noted. This should not be seen as a final work on this subject. It is meant to interest and entertain, and hopefully encourage others to continue the research and documentation.

A final note about which placenames were considered for the book. I decided to list post offices, school districts, and, from United States Geological Service quadrangle maps, watercourses, valleys, mountains, and other geographical features. I did not try to define, except superficially, street names. Such a listing will hopefully some day be available for every community in the county.

Finally, thank you to my wife, Colleen, and my children, Joseph and Ellen, who put up with many late nights of my typing and many references to new and wonderful discoveries of placename meanings. Colleen, as she has for many years, also served as my editor. Thank you, love.

— Mark Hall-Patton

About the Author

Mark Hall-Patton served as Curator and Director of the San Luis Obispo County Historical Museum from 1985 through 1993. He also wrote a weekly history column for the Telegraph-Tribune from 1987 through 1993. A fourth generation Californian, he has worked for various museums throughout the country since 1977. He is currently the Aviation Curator for the McCarran Aviation History Museum in Las Vegas, Nevada.

How To Use This Book

T his list of San Luis Obispo county placenames is designed to be used as a dictionary. All names are listed alphabetically. In most cases location information is not specifically given in the definition, except in the United States Geologic Service Quadrangle map listings, which are shown in parentheses ( ). The quadrangles used are all the 7.5 minute series, unless otherwise noted. These can be cross referenced with the map at the back of the book to locate names in their general vicinity.

The names given in brackets [ ] after some entries are the sources from which the information has been gleaned. The full title of those sources can be found in the bibliography.

Placenames of San Luis Obispo County

Abbott Canyon- Named for William Anderson Abbott, who ran horses in 1889 on his Little San Jose ranch where the canyon is located. (Wells Canyon)

Adelaida; post office, school district- The origin of this name has not been definitively established. An article in the San Luis Obispo Tribune noting the creation of the post office says it was named for the daughter of a neighbor of the new postmaster, Milton H. Sunderland. This was probably Adelaida Corelle, the daughter of Jose and Susana Corelle, who lived next door. Fraser MacGillivray, in his history of the area, lists three other possible explanations, in addition to the newspaper account. The post office operated from March 16, 1877 until December 31, 1936. The school district was founded in 1948 through the merger of the Lincoln and Sunderland school districts. (Adelaida)

Adobe Creek; canyon, flat, spring- The creek is in the San Simeon area, and the flat is on land which was part of the historic Godfrey Ranch. The flat is probably named for the original adobe buildings of the ranch. In the case of Adobe Canyon near Nipomo and Adobe Spring near Cholame, these were probably named for the presence of good adobe soil in the vicinity. Because of the importance of adobe as a building material in Spanish and early American California, over 75 places throughout the state are named for the material. [Gudde] (San Simeon/Oceano/ Santa Margarita/ Cholame)

Akmi; post office- Though this post office was established April 29, 1892, and not discontinued until October 29, 1894, postal service records state it was never in operation. A postmistress, Mrs. Elizabeth Hitchcock, was appointed though. I have not determined the origin of the name. [Salley]

Alamo; creek, school district- This is the Spanish word for a poplar or cottonwood tree, and was located on a part of the Rancho Huasna known as the Alamo. The school district was founded about 1895 and lapsed in 1929. See Cottonwood. (Huasna Peak/ Chimney Canyon/ Los Machos Hills)

Aliso Creek; canyon- In Spanish, this is an alder or sycamore tree. In California, the term was normally used for a sycamore. The creek is located near Suey Creek in the southern part of the county. (La Panza/ Los Machos Hills/ Chimney Canyon/ Miranda Pine Mountain)

Alliance; school district- Probably named for the Farmer's Alliance, a populist farmer's political party in the 1880's to the 1910's. The district was founded about 1894 at the peak of the Farmer's Alliance influence, and eventually merged with the Shandon district. The Farmer's Alliance was very strong in the area.

Alma; school district- This short lived school district was formed in 1901 and lapsed in 1913.

Almaden Flats- This was named for the Almaden Mine, a quicksilver mine in the area. (Pebblestone Shut-in)

Alta; school district- This school district was started in 1895 and joined the Polar Star district in 1902. The name is Spanish for high, and probably referred to its location in the coast range of mountains. In an interesting sidelight on names, Loren and Maude Thorndyke, who both grew up in the area, named their only daughter Alta after the school. [Thorndyke]

Alva Paul Creek- This was named for Alva Paul, a farmer whose farm was on the creek. (Morro Bay North)

American; canyon, canyon spring, school district- This possibly referred to the number of American settlers in the area. Most of the surrounding area was noted for its Mexican population. The school district was begun about 1890 and merged with Pozo in 1909. The canyon is above Pozo, and was used for sheep pasturage by Henry Ditmas, before being sold to Ned Douglas. (Pozo Summit/La Panza)

Amphibious Training Base; post office- This World War II training base takes its name from the use of the base as an amphibious training site for troops from Camp San Luis Obispo. It was located at Morro Bay, and was originally created as a Section Naval Base. It operated during 1944-45. The post office of this name was also known as Navy P.O. #10270, and was established February 7, 1944 as a branch of the Morro Bay Post Office. It was discontinued October 30, 1945.

Antelope Springs- Located on the Carrisa Plain, this is named for the pronghorn antelope which formerly inhabited the Carrisa Plain in great numbers.

Arroyo de la Cruz- In Spanish, this means creek or stream of the Holy Cross. Along this stream was the site of one of the Portolá expedition's camps. (San Simeon)

Arroyo de la Huerta Viejo- This means creek of the old garden and referred to the proximity of the creek to the Mission garden. This was an earlier name for today's Stenner Creek. See Stenner Creek.

Arroyo de la Laguna- This is Spanish for creek of the lake. (Piedras Blancas/ San Simeon)

Arroyo de los Chinos- above San Simeon, shown on the 1874 county map as above San Simeon, this means creek of the chinos. Chinos would normally translate as Chinese, though when used in Spanish America it could also refer to Indians and/or mestizos. If indeed it was named for Chinese, it would probably have been because of a kelp-drying operation in the area. I think, though, it is in the Indian meaning that this creek was named, as Indians still lived in the area in the 1870's. (Piedras Blancas)

Arroyo del Corral- In Spanish, this is creek of the corral, probably a location for holding, or rounding up, horses. It is also known as Arroyo Corral, and is located north of San Simeon on the coast. (Piedras Blancas)

Arroyo del Oso- In Spanish, this means creek of the bear, or bear creek. (Piedras Blancas)

Arroyo del Padre Juan- This creek is shown with this name on the 1874 County map. It refers to Father Juan Cabot, a priest at Mission San Miguel from 1807 to 1819, and again from 1824 to 1834. (Pico Creek/ Cambria/ Pebblestone Shut-in)

Arroyo del Pinal- This is probably a misspelling of Arroyo del Pinar, meaning creek of the pine forest. It is located south of Cambria.

Arroyo del Puerto, AKA Arroyo del Puerto de San Simeon- In Spanish, this means creek or stream of the port, a reference to San Simeon Bay. (San Simeon)

Arroyo Grande; Creek, valley, town, township, city, landgrant, school district- in Spanish, an arroyo grande is a big creek or stream. This refers to the creek and is first noted on the land grant of the Rancho Arroyo Grande or San Ramon to Zeferino Carlon on April 25, 1842. Parke-Custer recorded the name in 1855 [Gudde]. The township was established in 1862, and the town dates from about 1867. The school district was started before 1871. (Oceano/ Oceano OE W/ Arroyo Grande NE/ Tar Spring Ridge)

Selected Street Names in Arroyo Grande-

It should be noted that many street names given after 1960 by developer Kenneth Craig are a direct result of a conversation between him and Jean Hubbard in which she suggested that naming streets for historic figures in Arroyo Grande made more sense than for trees or flowers. Asked to make some suggestions, she and Gordon Bennett gave Craig over four pages of suggestions, many of which were used.

The big stream which gave the Arroyo Grande Rancho, and later the community, its name.

Allen- Perhaps named for Thomas Allen, an Arroyo Grande farmer.

Bennett- Named for Frank E. Bennett, first Mayor of Arroyo Grande.

Branch- Named for Francis Ziba Branch, grantee of the Santa Manuela Rancho on which the town was founded.

Branch Mill- Named for the grist mill of F.Z. Branch.

Bridge- Named for the bridge crossing the Arroyo Grande.

Brisco- Named for Leo Brisco, lumber mill owner and developer of the road.

Corbett Canyon- Named for John Corbit, early resident and blacksmith in town.

Fair Oaks- Named for the subdivision of this name. The

subdivision was given a real estate promotional name referring to the oaks in the area.

Felts Road- Today this road, named for John Felts, is called Royal Oak Road.

Halcyon- Named for the Halcyon Settlement. This road was originally called Cienega (swamp) in Spanish, as it was the road to the Cienega near today's Oceano.

Hawkins- Perhaps named for Arthur W. Hawkins, shown as a resident of Huasna in 1892.

Huasna- This was the road to the townsite of Huasna, which was named for the Huasna Land Grant. See Huasna.

Huebner- Named for J. Huebner, whose farm this road ran through. His brother farmed in the Los Berros area.

Ide- Named for Bela C. Ide, a blacksmith in Arroyo Grande.

James Way- This was originally the driveway to the homes of Dr. Arthur James and Glenn James, who were brothers. When the road was dedicated to the county, a name was needed and Glenn James noted they had always called it James Way. The driveway was later lengthened as subdivisions were built, becoming the major thorough-fare it is today.

Mason- Named for Charles J. Mason who married a daughter of John Rice, Myrtle Rice. John Rice built the two story yellow sandstone house in Arroyo Grande.

Myrtle- Named for Myrtle Rice, who became wife of Charles Mason.

Nelson- Named for Rev. C.W.F. Nelson, a pastor at the Methodist Church.

Poole- Named for James Poole, a local farmer.

Priscilla- Named for the granddaughter of Mr. McOscar, the developer of the area.

Ruthann- Named for the granddaughter of another resident of the area developed by McOscar, who felt his granddaughter deserved to be honored by a street also.

Short- Named for Newton Short, who also built the swinging bridge in downtown Arroyo Grande.

Tally Ho- Named for the Tally Ho Ranch of Horace A. Vachell, a prolific turn of the century English novelist who lived in our county for about 15 years.

Wesley- This road to the Methodist Campground is named for John Wesley, the founder of Methodism.

Whiteley- Named for Constable Whitely. His son, Thomas Whitely subdivided the Whitely addition to the town.

Arroyo Hondo- This creek is shown, misspelled as Arroyo Honda, on the 1874 County map as being near San Simeon. The name means deep creek in Spanish. (Piedras Blancas)

Arroyo Laguna- See Arroyo de la Laguna.

Arroyo Seco; creek, canyon, school district- In Spanish, this means dry creek. (Caldwell Mesa)

Arroyo Viejo- In Spanish, this means old creek. Today the creek is called Old Creek. See Old Creek.

Asuncion, Ascension; landgrant, SP siding, school district - In Spanish, this refers to the ascension of the Virgin Mary. A site called La Assumpcion was noted by Pedro Font in 1776. This was a rancho of the Mission San Luis Obispo, referred to as early as 1827 in mission records. The rancho was later granted to Pedro Estrada on June 19, 1845. The school district was founded before 1895. (Atascadero/ Santa Margarita/ Morro Bay North/ York Mountain/ Templeton/ Creston)

Atascadero; colony, city, lake, landgrant, school district - In Spanish, this means a bog or miry place. The landgrant was given to Trifon Garcia on May 6, 1842. The city, originally called the Atascadero Colony, was founded by E. G. Lewis in 1913. This was also the site of Camp Atascadero in 1904, 1908, and 1910. This was a summer encampment site for war games conducted by the regular Army and National Guard troops.

Selected Street Names in Atascadero

East Mall- Named for E.G. Lewis's planned mall which was to extend from the administration building to the high school.
Lewis- Named for the founder of Atascadero, Edward G. Lewis.
Morro- Named for Morro Bay. This was originally built to provide access to Lewis's Atascadero Beach development at Morro Bay.
Portola- Named for Gaspar de Portolá.

Atascadero Beach- This was a subdivision just north of Morro Bay developed by E. G. Lewis, as an adjunct to the City of Atascadero. It was the site of the famous hotel The Cloisters, which was demolished by the army during World War II. A portion of the beach is now called Morro Strand State Beach.

Avenal; post office, valley, school district- This post office, fifteen miles southeast of Pozo, was established on April 18, 1887. It was named for the valley, which in turn was named for the wild oats, or avena fatua, in the area.

Avenal means oat field in Spanish. The post office was discontinued May 15, 1905. The school district was founded in 1887 and lapsed in 1904.

Avila, Avila Beach; town, creek, hot springs, school district, rock - The town was subdivided in 1867 by the sons of Miguel Avila, grantee of the San Miguelito Rancho, and named in his honor. The school district was started in 1900, and consolidated with the Bellevue-Santa Fe district in 1966. The post office was started November 21, 1907. Beach was added to the post office name on June 1, 1955.

Bald Hill; knob, mountain- This is the third most popular name for mountains in our state. It refers to the lack of vegetation on the summit of the mountain. Bald Mountain was also known as Mt. Hasbrouck, in honor of Abram Hasbrouck who owned two celebrated ranches in the area, according to Myron Angel's history of our county. (Caldwell Mesa/ Lopez Mountain/ Port San Luis)

Banning; school district- Probably named for Mary Hollister Banning, the second wife of Phineas Banning, and daughter of John Hollister, who donated the land for the school. The district was created in 1896.

Basquez Creek- This is a misspelling of Vasquez Creek, named for Antonio Vasquez. See Vasquez Creek.

Bachelor's Hill- See Lodge Hill.

Battle Ground- This area near the Nacimiento River is named for the conflicts between sheepmen and home-steaders which took place in the area. [Adams] Another area with this name is located in the Upper Arroyo Grande valley, according to Madge Ditmas. It was named for a feud between early residents, where both parties were killed and not found for days. [Ditmas]

Bay-Osos; post office- Post office for the Baywood Park/ Los Osos area, established December 7, 1967 through the merger of the Baywood Park and part of the Los Osos post offices. Discontinued July 1, 1974. The name was never popular with local residents.

Baywood Park- This was a resubdivision of the Town of El Moro, a failed 1887 subdivision. The land was purchased and promoted by Walter Redfield in 1919. He used the names Redfield Acres and Redfield Woods for his developments. Later, with Richard Otto, the name Baywood Park was used, referring to the bay, or California laurel trees in the area.

Bear Canyon- According to Erwin Gudde's California Place Names, over 500 sites in California are named for the bear. In our county, in addition to Bear Canyon near Huasna, the Los Osos Valley and Beartrap Creek and Spring near La Panza all commemorate this well known indigenous animal.

Beck Lake- Located near Creston, this is named for the Beck family who owned land in the area. (Santa Margarita)

Bee Canyon- Bees have long been domestically used for their honey production, and even wild hives have been harvested. This canyon is probably named for hives in the vicinity. The canyon is also known as Deer Canyon. (Arroyo Grande)

Bee Rock Canyon; school district- This district was founded in 1887, and became part of the San Miguel district in 1945. The canyon was named by James Hardy Allen in 1881 for a large bee hive located in a rock. The long strips of honeycomb were visible until a fire destroyed them. [Adams/Stenner] A second Bee Rock Canyon is located in the Cuyama area in the extreme south of the county. (Tierra Redonda/ Wells Ranch/ New Cuyama)

Belle View/Belleview/Bellevue; school district- This school district was founded in 1883, and merged in 1946 with the Santa Fe district to become the Bellevue-Santa Fe district. (Pismo Beach)

Bellyache Spring- This is probably named for the quality of the water from the spring. (Holland Canyon)

Bern; post office- This post office and settlement was located six miles southeast of Estrella. It was established April 6, 1904, and discontinued February 29, 1932. It was named for the capitol of Switzerland.

Berros; creek, post office- Berros means watercress in Spanish, and was the name given to this creek on September 4, 1769 by Father Juan Crespi of the Portolá expedition. The creek was noted for the abundance of watercress in the water. The watercress was important as it prevented scurvy. The first post office was established on February 8, 1870, and discontinued on May 6, 1872. A post office was re-established as Los Berros on March 30, 1888, after the townsite was subdivided and promoted during the boom of the late 1880's. The post office's name was changed to Berros on July 13, 1901, and discontinued November 30, 1920. Re-established on August 3, 1921, the post office was finally discontinued May 15, 1940. The town was never very successful, but the Los Berros school district existed from 1891 until it merged with Arroyo Grande in 1944.

Bethel; school district- This school district was founded before 1895 and merged with the Encinal district in 1946, which later became part of the Paso Robles district. It

Los Berros, as shown in 1894. This is one of San Luis Obispo county's placenames which survives from the Gaspar de Portola Expedition of 1769

probably took its name from the Bethel Lutheran Church, which was started by the Swedish residents of the area in 1887. The name was used for the entire area before the school district was founded. (Templeton)

Big Baldy- This mountain is named for the absence of trees on the summit. See Bald. (Tar Spring Ridge)

Big Falls Canyon- This canyon in the Santa Lucia wilderness, is named for a large water fall in the canyon. (Lopez Mountain)

Big Pocket Lake- One of the dune lakes located in the Oceano Dunes, it is named for its shape. (Oceano)

Big Twin Lake/ Small Twin Lake- These two dune lakes are named for their proximity to each other. (Oceano)

Bird Rock- Named for the number of birds which congregate on this rock, it is a landmark in Pismo Beach. It is located between the northbound and southbound lanes of Highway 101. It was a site for picnics and camping the late 19th century. It has also been known as Sea Gull and Gull Rock. There is also a rock off the coast of Pismo Beach with this name, named again for the number of birds on the rock. (Pismo Beach)

Bishop, Bishop's Peak- The name of this peak in Spanish was Cerro Obispo, which translates to Bishop Peak. It is known by both the possessive and the singular of the name. It takes its name from the similarity of the top of the mountain to the top of a bishop's miter, or hat. (San Luis Obispo)

Bitterwater Creek; canyon, valley- Located on the north side of the Carrisa Plain, this is a common form of placename in California's dry regions. According to Gudde, there are more than 50 such names in the state. The relative palatability of water is of great concern in such areas. (La Panza/ Packwood Creek/ Orchard Peak/ Shale Point/ Holland Canyon)

Bitumina; Pacific Coast Railway siding- This siding on the Pacific Coast Railway near Edna was developed for the moving of bituminous earth which was quarried nearby. It was located near the Edna Valley end of Price Canyon. Many streets in San Luis Obispo, Walnut Creek, Santa Barbara and other communities were paved with bituminous earth from these quarries.

Black- This adjective is the most common color adjective used in place names in California. In our county we have Black Butte (near Lopez Lake), Black Hill (one of the peaks running from San Luis Obispo to Morro Bay), Black Lake (shown as Laguna Negra on the county map of 1874 and one of the Dune Lakes, as well as a canyon the lake is in and a school district which formerly included the area), Black Mountain, Black Spring (Holland Canyon), Black Sulphur Spring (Caliente Mountain), and Black Rock (off Cayucos Point). It is normally applied because of the dark color of the site or something noted about the lake. The Black Lake school district was begun in 1887, and merged with Arroyo Grande in 1920.

Blinn Spring- This was likely named for Oscar and Anita Blinn, who arrived in this area about 1900. (Camatta Ranch)

Blockman Valley- Probably named for Blockman, a partner with Cerf in the general mercantile business in San Luis Obispo. They were co-owners of a gold mining operation in this area, in addition to their other businesses.

Boar Peak- Located near Huasna Peak, this is named for the wild boar which were common in the area. (Huasna Peak)

Bolsa Chica Lake- One of the dune lakes. In Spanish this means small pocket, as in a pocket of land surrounded on three sides by water. In this case, it probably refers to the lake being relatively inaccessible. (Oceano)

Bolsa de Chamisal; landgrant- This is a Spanish name which means pocket of chaparral or brushwood. It refers to the overgrown nature of the land within much of this landgrant. The 'bolsa' part of the name refers to a pocket in the sense of a partially surrounded area, often referring to a neck of land surrounded by a swamp or lake. Chamisal is more correctly the white-flowering greasewood, but was used in placenames for chaparral. The land grant was given to Francisco Quijada on May 11, 1837.

Bootlegger Flat- Located in the Adelaida area, this was named for a large bootlegging operation located here in the early twentieth century. A small mountain of empty bottles, and various unidentified pieces of the stills, are still on the flat. [Blyth]

Bowman Spring- Probably named for the Bowman family. Ione MacLean Bowman, sister of Angus (Othor) MacLean, was a well-known artist, who illustrated all of her brother's books on the early history and tales of the county's back country. (La Panza)

Branch; mountain, lookout, creek, school district- Francis Ziba Branch was the grantee of the Rancho Santa Manuela on April 6, 1837. The school district, which was on his land, is named in his honor. It was founded in 1876. (Branch Mountain)

Brickton; Southern Pacific (SP) station- This station is shown as 1 mile north of Atascadero's station in the 1918 SP station list. It was named for a brickyard started by E.G. Lewis. [Krieger]

Bridge Canyon- Located near San Miguel, this canyon is probably named for the Bridge family, who ranched in the area. (Paso Robles)

Brizzolara, Brizziolari Creek- Named for Bartolo Brizzolara who was born in 1824 and married Adelaida

Francis Ziba Branch, grantee of the Santa Manuela Rancho, whose name is preserved in a mountain, creek, lookout, and school district.

Price in 1866. He was one of the founders of the Josephine Mining Company and died in 1881. He owned the ranch through which the creek ran. The creek was earlier known as the Arroyo del Portrero, or creek of the pasture, taking its name from the Rancho Portrero del San Luis Obispo. The variant spelling is listed on the Geographic Names Inventory of the U. S. Geologic Service, but its origin is unclear. [Stechman] (SLO)

Bromela; SP siding- This is a named siding on the Southern Pacific line, and is located near Oso Flaco lake. The origin of the name is unclear. (Oceano)

Brunswick Canyon- Near McMillan canyon, this was probably named for James McMillan's previous home in New Brunswick, Canada. McMillan Canyon was earlier known as New Brunswick Canyon.

Buchon; point, mountain, landing (see Spooner's Cove)- In Spanish, buchon means goiter, and this name was given by men of the Portolá expedition to a local Chumash Chief because of the goiter on his neck. The name was applied by the expedition to the valley now known as Price Canyon, as well as Port San Luis and the Santa Lucias, which were noted as Bahia de Buchon and Sierra de Buchon. Today it is the name of a mountain and a point along our coast. (Port San Luis Obispo)

Burnett Canyon; peak, camp- Named for the Wesley Burnett family who leased land in the area from Juan Castro, who had married the widow of Mariano Pacheco. (San Simeon)

Burnt Well- Named for a camp fire which escaped the confines of the fire circle and burned the redwood pulley which was used to get water from this well. The well is located on the Carrisa Plain. [White]

C **aballada Creek-** This may be a corruption of cabalgadar, Spanish for riding on horseback. (Pebblestone Shut-in/ Bryson)

Cabrillo Heights- Developer name for the subdivision near Montaña de Oro. Mr. Rodman, the developer was a Texan, and most of the streets are named for historical Texas people, with the exception of the street he named for himself.

Caldwell Mesa; mountain- Named for a Mr. Caldwell who had a partner named Barnhill. Lived in the Huasna area. [Porter] (Caldwell Mesa)

Caliente Range; mountain- Spanish for hot, this range was not named for the hot, dry weather of the area according to Gudde. Instead, it was named for a nearby hot spring, the Ojo Caliente, noted on the Parke-Custer map of 1855. (Wells Ranch/ Caliente Mountain)

California Valley; post office, townsite- This is a real estate development on the Carrisa Plain, originally promoted in 1960. It is a subdivision of the El Chicote, or grass rope, Ranch. The post office was established May 16, 1963, and was discontinued June 30, 1974. It was not a successful effort, though sales continue of some of the lots and the subdivision continues in force. (California Valley)

Callender; settlement, SP siding- Named for C. R. Callender who was involved with promoting eucalyptus growing on the Nipomo Mesa. He subdivided and promoted the town of Los Berros. Callender built a hotel at

Camatti Ranch, main buildings about 1880. Photo courtesy Harold Miossi.

the site of the siding in the late teens.

Camatta Canyon; creek- This name derives from a Salinan/Chumash border village named Camate, as shown in the San Miguel Mission records. Another, more fanciful, explanation is that it is named for the Spanish word for comet. The area was part of the San Juan Capistrano del Camate land grant of 10 leagues. This grant, made in 1846 to Trineo Herrera and Geronimo Quintana, was not accepted by the Land Courts under the American government, and the lands were opened to settlers. Other spellings for this area include Comate, Comatti, La Cometa, Comata, Camata, Commatti, Cammatta, Commatta, Commatri. [Farris] (Camatta Ranch/ Pozo)

Cambria; post office, town, rock, school district- Originally founded as Rosaville, named for the Santa Rosa Creek. When the first post office was applied for the name was rejected by the post office department. Since there was a San Simeon post office in the area, it was moved to the new town. This met with disfavor with the local residents, and a new name was sought. Dr. Frame, a Welsh doctor, is credited with suggesting the name based on his homeland's name of Cambria, based on the reminiscences of Mrs. Elsie Loose, granddaughter of pioneer Cambria resident Needham Gillespie. Another claimant for the honor of having named the new community is a Mr. Llewellyn, another Welsh resident of the area. Geneva Hamilton, in Where the Highway Ends, claims the honor is due P. A. Forrester, who suggested the name based on a community of the same name in Pennsylvania which was located in a similar natural setting. Still another explana-

An overview of Cambria about 1890. The honor of having named Cambria has been claimed by and for many over the years.

tion is noted in Gudde, where he relates that a carpenter named Llewellyn named his shop the Cambria Carpentry Shop for his native Wales. It should be noted that there was a John Presnell Lewelling living in the area, but he is listed as a native of the United States and a farmer in the Great Registers of 1867 and 1871. It will probably never be known positively to whom is due the honor. The post office department accepted the new name and the post office became Cambria on January 10, 1870. Most streets in Cambria are named for places in England, and reflect the British heritage of many of the twentieth century residents of the town. (Cambria)

Camp Atascadero- see Atascadero

Camp Natoma; youth camp- This may be related to the Natoma in Sacramento County, which is often translated as clear water. According to Kroeber, however, this is only fanciful thinking by Americans, and the word is related to the Maidu word nato/noto, meaning north or up river. It was probably a village name. (Lime Mountain)

Camp Roberts- This army training camp was originally named Camp Nacimiento, after the ranch it was built on, but when officially opened, it was named for Corporal Harold D. Roberts, a World War 1 Medal of Honor winner. It was the first army camp in the United States named for an enlisted man. It opened in March of 1941 and closed in 1946. It reopened in July 1950 to train men for the Korean War, and stayed an active Army training camp until 1971, when the California National Guard took over the camp under a 25 year lease.

Camp San Luis Obispo- This was a national guard summer encampment site founded in 1928. It was renamed Camp Merriam for a short time by Governor Frank Merriam in 1934, but was quickly renamed Camp San Luis Obispo after a public outcry. In 1940 it was activated as a regular army training camp, training nearly 500,000 men during World War II. Deactivated in 1946, it was reactivated during the Korean War. After the Korean War the camp was returned to the California National Guard. Much of the land acquired before and during World War II, when the camp was expanded, has been used for other purposes, including Cuesta College, the expansion of Cal Poly San Luis Obispo, the California Men's Colony, and various County facilities. The core of the land is still an active California National Guard Training base. There was a post office on the base from December 15, 1940 until January 31, 1948, and again from January 2, 1952 until April 15, 1957.

Cañada de los Coches- This means canyon of the carriages or coaches in Spanish. (Twitchell Dam)

Cañada de los Osos y Pecho y Islay; landgrant- The landgrant takes its name from two previous landgrants, which were combined into this 32,000 acre plus gift to James Scott and John Wilson. The Cañada de los Osos was named by the men of the Portolá expedition for the number of California grizzly bears found in the valley. See Los Osos, Pecho, Islay.

Cañada de Trigo- In Spanish, this means canyon of wheat. See Lopez Canyon.

Cañada Verde- See Verde

Cañon/Canyon; school district- Named for its location in See Canyon. The schoolhouse was located in the center of the canyon. The district was founded before 1882 and merged with the Bellevue-Santa Fe district after 1946.

Cantinas Creek; school district- The school district was founded in 1887, and lapsed in 1901. The name in Spanish means canteen or winecellar. (Bryson)

Canyon de Los Alisos- In Spanish, alisos are alder or sycamore trees. There are a number of geographic sites in San Luis Obispo county which are named for sycamore trees, including two Sycamore Canyons and Sycamore Hot Springs. (Arroyo Grande)

Carisa; post office- See Carrisa Plain

Carnaza Creek; spring- This is probably derived from carne, meaning flesh. In Carneceria and Carnicero, the word is used in the sense of a meat market or butcher. (La Panza Ranch/ La Panza NE)

Carneros Canyon; creek- The Carneros Rocks took their name from the canyon, which was named because of the use of the area's natural corrals to hold cattle for slaughter. This canyon has also been called MacLean Canyon. (Las Yeguas/ Carneros Rocks)

Carpenter Canyon- Named for the Ezra Carpenter family. Carpenter served as county surveyor from 1879 to 1881, and again from 1884 to 1885. (Arroyo Grande NE)

Carrizo/Carrisa Plain/Plains; valley, post office- The term carrisa or carrizo refers to the carrizo grass, a bunch grass or reed which was noted by early explorers in the valley. The grass was important to the Chumash because a sweetener, panoche, was made from it. The first post office to carry this name was spelled Carisa, and was operated from July 29, 1882 until December 29, 1888. The name was changed to Painted Rock (see Painted Rock) on that date. A second post office was established on February 29, 1916 as Carissa Plain, operating until December 30, 1916. Local spelling has varied over the years with one or two r's and one or two s's, but I have chosen to agree with the San Luis Obispo Tribune's decision of the 1890's to spell the name with two r's and one s. The spelling with two "r"s and a "z" is the one listed on USGS Quadrangle maps. The plain has been called the carrisa plains until fairly recently, when the carrizo spelling, and the "s" on plain was standardized on maps. (California Valley/ Painted Rock/ Elkhorn Hills/ Wells Ranch/ Caliente Mountain/ Panorama Hills/ Chimineas Ranch/ McKittrick Summit/ Simmler/ La Panza NE)

Carrizo Canyon- Refers to the carrizo grass found in the canyon. (Taylor Canyon/ Chimineas Ranch)

Cashin Station- Named for Thomas Cashin, who ran this stagecoach stop from 1873 until 1883. Cashin was from Ireland. The station was sold to Sheerin. See Sheerin's Station. [Tribune, 4/23/1915]

Castle Crags- Located in the La Panza district, this formation is named for its resemblance to a castle. (La Panza)

Castle Rock; school district- This district was split off from the Oak Grove district in 1895, and changed its name to Nacimiento in 1906. It takes its name from a rock formation in the area.

Castro Canyon- As below, named for early resident Francisco Castro, an early Sheriff of San Luis Obispo county. (Pismo Beach)

Castro's Station- This was the terminus of the Pacific Coast Railroad in 1875. It was located west of the Bellevue-Santa Fe Schoolhouse near the San Luis Creek Bridge on Highway 101. It takes its name from Francisco Castro who owned property next to the station. This was the site of the townsites of Harford and Monte, and was also known as Miles Station. This was also the site of the later post office of Root. See Root, Miles Station, Monte, Harford.

Cave Landing- This was the first landing at Port San Luis, or San Luis Bay. It was utilized during the Mission, Mexican and early American periods of our County's history. It takes its name from a natural cave at the beach. It has also been known as Mallagh's Landing, because David Mallagh's Wharf was located at this site. In the early 1960's, treasure hunters decided that this was the site where Sir Francis Drake buried his treasure, and the term Pirate's Cove came in to use for the site. It should be noted that this was without any historical validity, and no pirates are ever known to have landed at the site. Today, this is the only clothing-optional beach in San Luis Obispo County. (Pismo Beach)

Caverns of Mystery/Wonder- see Dinosaur Caves.

Cayucos, Cayucas; bay, town, school district, creek, point- This name is a Spanish version of the Eskimo word kayak. A Cayuco is described in Font's diaries in 1776. The term was early applied to this area of our county, and was well established when the Cayucos land grant was given to Vicente Feliz on April 27, 1842. This land grant was later combined with the Moro when the land was patented to James McKinley on January 19, 1878. The town's origin came in 1867, with the arrival of James Cass. The post office was established as Cayucas on January 18, 1879, and changed to Cayucos on February 28, 1883. (Cayucos)

Cedar Spring; canyon- Located near San Miguel, the canyon is named for the spring, which was probably named for cedar trees in the area. Cedars give their name to over 100 placenames throughout California. (La Panza Ranch)

Celery Lake- This dune lake is named for the large amount of celery grown in the area. (Oceano)

Cemetery Hill- Located south of San Luis Obispo, this is named for the Catholic Cemetery at the base of the hill. The cemetery was moved here in the 1870's, when it was considered bad for the community to have a cemetery in the middle of downtown. The land was marsh land and not good for planting or grazing. Most of the white burials from the Mission cemetery were moved to this new cemetery, and most of the neophyte or Indian burials were left next to the Mission. These were eventually removed by roadwork and church expansion. [Krieger]

Central; school district- This district was founded before 1871 and became part of the Cayucos district in 1942. Its name may have come from its location between the Franklin and Excelsior school districts, out of which it was formed.

Cerro Alto- This means high, or difficult, mountain in Spanish. Though Hollister Peak was once known by this name as well, the Cerro Alto which retains this name in our county is along the west Cuesta ridge. That peak was known by this name on USGS Quadrangle maps by 1897. See Hollister Peak. (Atascadero)

Cerro Cabrillo- Named for Juan Rodriguez Cabrillo at the suggestion of then Curator of the San Luis Obispo County Historical Museum, Louisiana Clayton Dart, in 1964. AKA Cabrillo Peak (Morro Bay South)

Cerro Obispo- Spanish for Bishop Peak. See Bishop Peak. (San Luis Obispo)

Cerro Romualdo- This peak took its name from the Huerto de Romualdo Rancho at its base. See Huerto de Romualdo. (San Luis Obispo)

Cerro San Luis- See San Luis Mountain. (San Luis Obispo)

Chalk Mountain- Named for the chalky stone found on the mountain. (Caliente Mountain)

Chanslor; SP siding- This is named for J.A. Chanslor, owner of the Stone Canyon Coal Mine before Hood McKay. This station was renamed McKay. It is located north of San Miguel. See McKay. (Adams)

Cheapskate Hill- Located next to Cemetery Hill outside of San Luis Obispo, this hill overlooked the old racetrack in Exposition Park. It is named for those people who viewed the races without paying the entrance fee.

Chico Martinez Creek- Named for Chico Martinez, the 'king of the mustang runners.' Martinez was noted for his stone corral, built near the creek to hold the wild mustangs he hunted. [Rensch-Hoover/Darling]

Chimney Rock- Named for its resemblance to a chimney, it is located on the ranch of the same name. (Adelaida)

China Gulch- Name given to the small creek above the site of the Washington School in the San Simeon area, it was named for Chinese residents in the area. [Thorndyke]

China Harbor; point- Named for the Chinese residents of this point. How Wong and his uncle maintained a residence here for over a century. (Cayucos)

Choice Valley; school district- The school district was begun in 1890. The valley was named for its fine location. (Orchard Peak/ Holland Canyon)

Cholame; town, post office, landgrant, creek, valley, school district- This landgrant's name was taken from a Salinan or Yokut village name, first shown as Cholaam. It has been variously spelled Cholan, Cholama, Chollame, Cholami, Choloma, Cholamen and Cholam, the accepted spelling today is Cholame. The post office was established on May 14, 1873, and discontinued on March 31, 1908. It was re-established on December 8, 1908. The landgrant was given to Mauricio Gonzales on February 7, 1844. The meaning of the name is uncertain. The school district was begun before 1895. (Cholame)

Chorro; landgrant, valley, creek, townsite, SP station, street(SLO)- In Spanish, this term means rapids, or small waterfall. The Arroyo del Chorro is shown on the diseño of the Huerta de Romualdo o del Chorro Rancho. This landgrant's earliest records shows it with the El Chorro name, but is known today as the Huerta de Romualdo. The creek also gave its name to the valley and to the Cañada del Chorro landgrant, given to James Scott and John Wilson on October 10, 1845. The Chorro townsite was originally called Goldtree, and was located at the Goldtree siding on the Southern Pacific Railroad. Chorro Street in the City of San Luis Obispo takes its name form the fact that it was the road to the Chorro Valley. See Huerta de Romualdo. (San Luis Obispo)

Chris Flood Creek- Named for Chris Flood, an early twentieth century resident who had a small cattle ranch on the creek. [Thorndyke] (Burro Mountain/ Burnett Peak)

Chumash Peak- Named in honor of the Chumash Indians of the county at the suggestion of then-Curator of the San Luis Obispo County Historical Museum Louisiana Dart in 1964. (San Luis Obispo)

Cienega; road, school district, valley, creek- Spanish for marsh, this was applied to the Pacific end of the Arroyo Grande valley. This was a marshy district. The school district was begun in 1888 and lapsed in 1919. The creek by this name is located in the Cypress Mountain area, and is not related to the valley. (Oceano)

Clark Valley- Named for Joseph Clark Welsh, an early settler. (Morro Bay South)

Clarke Canyon; park- The canyon and community park in Shandon were named for Crawford W. Clarke, pioneer resident of the area. The park was donated by his daughter, Mrs. Baldwin. (Estrella/ Shandon/ Cholame Hills)

Coal Mountain- This peak north of Cambria acquired its name from the coal deposits found on its slopes. No deposits of commercial size were ever located.

Coasta District- This was the original name for the north coast Supervisorial district in the 1850's. It refers to the location of the district.

College Hill- This hill near Templeton takes its name from the Templeton Institute, a private school run for a short time by Reverend J. D. E. Summers soon after the town was founded in 1887.

Comatti Canyon- See Camatta Canyon.

Coon Creek; canyon- This was probably named for raccoon found in the area. This name is given to over 50 places in California. [Gudde] (Port San Luis/ Morro Bay

South)

Corbett/Corbit Canyon- Named for John Corbit, or Corbett, a pioneer blacksmith in Arroyo Grande. This canyon's name was originally spelled Corbit, but was changed for unknown reasons after John Corbit's death in 1912. [Olsen] (Oceano/ Arroyo Grande NE)

Coreopsis Hill- Named for the spectacular giant coreopsis plants on the hill, this is located in the Nipomo Dunes.

Corral de los Mulos- This name in the Adelaida region refers to a corral for mules, and shows on the early maps of our county. It may refer to a Mission era mule raising area. [Macgillivray]

Corral de Piedra; creek, landgrant, school district- This landgrant was named for its stone corrals (Corral de Piedra), and was given to Jose Maria Villavicencia on May 14, 1841. The rancho was originally a Mission rancho, used for rounding up wild cattle. The stone corrals had been built by the Indians at the Mission, and they unsuccessfully requested this rancho during secularization. The creek takes its name from the corrals, and the school district, founded before 1882 and merged into the Los Ranchos school in 1959, from the rancho.

Corralitos Valley; canyon- This means little corrals in Spanish. (Arroyo Grande NE)

Cottonwood Canyon; spring, pass, well- Many sites in the county are named for the cottonwood tree, either in English or in its Spanish version, alamo. According to

Gudde, it is a favorite placename in California. (Pyramid Hills/ Tent Hills/ Caliente Mountain/ Las Yeguas/ Orchard Peak)

Coyote; hole, point- The word coyote is taken from the Aztec words for a prairie wolf. It was a popular placename in California, and at least two places in our county carry the name. In addition to the animal, in Mexican California the term referred to a half-breed. During the gold rush, it was also used to refer to a type of mining where the hole was dug in the ground and the dirt thrown around the opening to the shaft. (La Panza/ Atascadero)

Creston; town, lake, post office, school district- This town was subdivided and promoted by Thomas Ambrose, Amos Adams, J.V. Webster, and C. J. Cressy in 1884. The town was named for Cressy, and its four major streets for the four partners. The post office was established on January 26, 1885 and the school district in the same year.

Crookshank's Creek- Above San Simeon, this was named for an early miner who found a small gold mine along the creek. [Thorndyke]

Cuesta; pass, school district, college, SP siding- In Spanish, cuesta means grade. This is a descriptive term for the pass north of San Luis Obispo on Highway 101. This pass was a difficult grade for the padres, the stagecoaches, the railroad, and continues to be the worst grade on Highway 101. The La Cuesta Rancho was claimed by Jose Maria Bonilla, though this claim was not upheld by the land courts in American California. The land was then acquired by the Goldtrees. Later the ranch was owned by

The Cuesta, Spanish for grade, about 1885. The road shown is the 1876 Stagecoach road built by the County. It was superceded in 1915 by the original version of today's Highway 101 route.

Tate, who sold to the Miossi family. The SP siding was listed as early as 1894 in the SP station listing, and was noted as the summit. The school district, founded before 1895 and merged with the Independence district in 1921, and college take their name from the grade. Named La Cuesta in 1937 by the California Division of Highways, today Cal Trans has a sign at the top of the grade reading Cuesta Grade, a redundancy. [Miossi] (San Luis Obispo)

Cuesta by the Sea- This was a real estate promotion on land which had been the dairy farm of John and Maggie McGinnis. It was acquired by I. L. Mitchell, who subdivided the land and renamed it. Its major promoter was Arthur Coleman. (Morro Bay South)

Cushing; SP station- This station is listed as two miles north of Santa Margarita in the June 1955 Southern Pacific timetable. The source of the name is unknown to the author. (Santa Margarita)

Cuyama; valley, landgrants, post office, school district-This name was taken from the Chumash word Kuyam or Kuya'am, meaning to rest or wait. The name was utilized for two landgrants, Cuyama 1 and Cuyama 2, given in 1843 and 1846 respectively, but first appears on a map in 1824 as the name of the Arroyo Llamado de Cuyam. It was the name of a village in the area. The post office was established on July 11, 1916, but never operated. It was re-established on April 18, 1942. A second community, in Santa Barbara County, was named New Cuyama, with a post office established on July 16, 1953. The valley is in both San Luis Obispo and Santa Barbara counties. The school district was founded in 1910 and merged with the Nipomo district in 1945. (Miranda Pine Mountain/ Taylor Canyon/ Caliente Mountain/ Peak Mountain/ New Cuyama/ Cuyama/ Fox Mountain/ Ballinger Canyon)

Cypress Mountain- Named for the Sargent Cypress, found on the west Cuesta ridge. [Gudde/Miossi] (Cypress Mountain)

Pablo de la Guerra, for whom De La Guerra Canyon, location of the County's 1878-79 gold rush , was named.

Dairy Creek- Named for the Guidetti, Walter and Gilardi dairies, through which this creek ran. [Miossi] (San Luis Obispo)

Davidson Seamount- This underwater mountain is located off Morro Bay. It was named for George Davidson, who was a member of the first California Geological Survey. It was named in 1938, after having been located in 1932. According to the Geographic Board, which named the formation, this was the first use of the term seamount, because existing terms such as bank, shoal and pinnacle were inappropriate. [Gudde] According to one account, this was earlier known as Church Rock, after an early pilot for ships coming in at Morro Bay. Church was a contemporary of Rev. Spooner. [Ahrendt]

Davis Canyon; Peak- The canyon was probably named for the peak, as no Davis family ever lived in the canyon, according to local researcher Judy Chambers. The name appears on the 1895 USGS Quad. (Pismo Beach/ Port San Luis)

Dawson Grade- Located on the south road into Cambria, this may be named for Thomas Dawson, resident and registered voter in Cambria in 1892. (Cambria)

De La Guerra Canyon- This was the canyon where the La Panza Gold rush of the late 1870's started. Unfortunately, it is not known today which of the canyons in the area carried this name. It was named for Pablo de la Guerra.

Dead Man Flat- An area near the mouth of the San Juan Capistrano creek where a horse thief was lynched and the body left hanging. [O'Donovan] (Chimineas Ranch)

Dead Man's Point- Small point on the south end of Cayucos, named for a man who camped on the land and died in his sleep. He was found the next day, under his wagon. [Thorndyke]

Deep Hole- This is where the Nacimiento Dam is today, and was called this at the turn of the century. It was a noted fishing spot. [Stanley]

Deer Canyon; flat, spring- Only bear outranks deer as a favorite placename in California. In our county there are two Deer Canyons, one Deer Flat, and one Deer Spring. Deer Flat was near Lynch in the north county, and was an area where James Lynch ran sheep. [Gudde] (Port San Luis/ Huasna/ Pebblestone Shut-in/ Wilson Corner)

Del Mar Heights, Del Mar-Heights- A real estate promotional name, this was also the name of a rural station post office of Morro Bay from May 1, 1953 until July 31,

1972. It was originally spelled with the hyphen, which was dropped in 1966. It means of the sea in Spanish. (Morro Bay North)

Deleissigues Creek- Named for the family of Captain Oliver Deleissigues. He was born about 1800, and eventually settled in San Luis Obispo. His daughter Justina married Francis Dana, and it is perhaps for her specifically that the creek is named. (Nipomo)

Devil's Gap- This ragged, rocky gorge is named for the forbidding nature of the terrain. It is on Highway 41 between Morro Bay and Atascadero. (Atascadero)

Diablo Canyon- Diablo is Spanish for devil. The canyon was named long before it became a household name with the building of the nuclear power plant in the area. (Port San Luis)

Dinosaur Caves- This tourist attraction at Shell Beach was a route to the beach by the turn of the century. It was developed in the 1920's as a tourist attraction, under various names including Caverns of Mystery and Pismo Caves. H. Douglas Brown began to build a cement dinosaur next to the entrance to the caves in 1948, but was stopped by local opposition before it was finished, leaving the dinosaur headless. The headless dinosaur was a local landmark until the late 1950's, when it was destroyed. (Pismo Beach)

Douglas Spring; canyon- Located in the La Panza area, this may have been named for Thomas Douglas, resident of the area in 1892. (Pozo Summit)

Dove- This townsite, now part of Atascadero, probably took its name from Paloma Creek. Paloma means dove or pigeon in Spanish. The Southern Pacific Railroad's Hazel station was at this location.

Dover Canyon- Named for James Dover, shown as resident on the creek on the 1874 County Map. (York Mountain)

Dry Canyon- Two canyons in this county bear this name, as well as one creek which lent its name to a school district. Dry is used for over 100 creeks and over 25 lakes in California. In most cases, the areas were named during the dry season, as few are dry year round. The school district was formed in 1883, and merged with Paso Robles in 1919. (Estrella/ Huasna Peak/ Creston/ Shedd Canyon/ Tar Spring Ridge)

Dughi Spring- Probably named for the Giovachini Dughi family of San Luis Obispo, which also owned property on Chorro Street. (San Luis Obispo)

Dutra Creek- Near San Carpojo Creek, this is named for the Dutra family.

E agle; school district- This school district was begun about 1886, and became part of the Shandon district in 1924. The district was probably named for the Eagle Ranch of Baron Von Schroeder. (Atascadero)

Eagle Peak; creek- Baron Von Schroeder named his Eagle Ranch for a pair of eagles which nested on this peak. An alternate explanation for the name is in an article published in the Tribune on March 30, 1883. It reports that the Baron had, during the summer of 1882, captured an eaglet in a nest on the side of this mountain and raised it, taking it eventually to San Francisco. In either case, the eagle gave the peak, creek and ranch their name. (Atascadero)

Eaglet; SP siding, community- Named for Eagle Ranch, Baron Von Schroeder's ranch southwest of Atascadero, this station was two miles south of Atascadero.

East Santa Fe; school district- The school district was begun in 1876, and merged with the Corral de Piedra and Independence districts in 1959 to become the Los Ranchos school. It was east of the Santa Fe district and the Ranchita Santa Fe.

Edna; post office, town- The post office of Edna was established on June 7, 1887, with Lynferd Maxwell as postmaster. Seven years later, Maxwell laid out a town at the site of the post office which he called Maxwellton. The new name never caught on, and the town took the name of the post office. Who Edna was has never been fully established. Maxwell's first granddaughter was named

Edna, and may have been the source of the name. Another claimant was Edna Laurel Clark Calhan, daughter of Charles H. Clark. Her claim was that the town was named for her at her father's suggestion. As is often the case with such names, there may never be a definitive answer. The post office was discontinued on September 30, 1920. See Maxwellton. (Arroyo Grande NE)

Eight Mile House- This stage stop was located eight miles north of San Luis Obispo on the old stage road, hence the name. It was operated by the Bean Brothers, Reuben and Edwin. It was also known as the Bean Brothers Hotel.

El Dorado/Eldorado; school district- This district was founded before 1882, and lapsed in 1947. It was later merged into the Pozo district. I was probably named because of the short lived La Panza gold rush. El Dorado means the golden, and refers to the legendary country of the gilded king.

Elkhorn; hills, plain, valley, grade, scarp, school district- Named for the many tule elk horns found in the area by early settlers. The school district was founded in 1918, and merged with the Simmler district in 1928. (Elkhorn Hills/ Wells Ranch/ Maricopa)

El Moro- This townsite was laid out in 1888, and a map of the town was deposited with the County in April 1889. It was developed by E. B. Whitney, and was one of the failed townsites of the late 1880's boom in the county. Later, parts of the townsite were acquired by Richard Otto and Walter Redfield and developed as Los Osos and Baywood Park.

El Pomar- An area between Templeton and Creston noted for its fruit and almond growing, this means the orchard in Spanish.

Encinal; school district- Spanish for the live or evergreen oak. The district was founded before 1895, and merged with the Bethel district in 1936.

Eocene; SP station- The eocene is the earliest epoch of the Tertiary Period of geologic history, and the geological strata where most oil is found. This station was located one mile north of the Paso Robles station, and is shown in the 1918 SP station listing.

Estero; bay, point, school district- Named by Father Juan Crespi on September 9, 1769, as Estero de Santa Serafina, the name has been shortened to Estero Bay. This is the bay which runs from Point Estero (named for the bay) to Point Buchon, and includes Cayucos and Morro Bay. Estero means estuary in Spanish, and has also been spelled Estros and Esteros. The school district was founded in 1873, and merged with the Morro district in 1893. (Cayucos/ Morro Bay/ Morro Bay South/ Morro Bay South OE W)

Estrada Creek- Named for Jose Ramon Estrada, grantee of the Rancho San Simeon. (Burro Mountain/ Burnett Peak)

Estrada Garden- Joaquin Estrada built his home here after losing his Rancho Santa Margarita. It was a noted local showplace, and a well known picnic site for local residents. The old adobe was bulldozed about 1974, and most of the roof tiles used to roof a new building at the

Rios-Caledonia Adobe in San Miguel. Most of the beautiful foliage was lost in the Las Pilitas Fire of 1985. Only a few palm trees and an orchard planted by H. Mehlmann, a later owner of the site, mark the area at the foot of the Cuesta. (San Luis Obispo)

Estrada Ridge- Named for Julian Estrada, grantee of the Santa Rosa Rancho in 1844. He built his home on the east slope of this ridge. [GNIS] (Cambria)

Estrella; post office, school district, church, river- This means star in Spanish. It first appears on the diseño of San Miguel in 1840, as the name for the creek. In 1844 it was applied to a grant of lands to the neophytes of Mission San Miguel, but this grant was not confirmed by the United States. The town is shown as early as G.H. Derby's map of 1850. The post office was established July 8, 1888, and discontinued on August 15, 1918. The school district was founded before 1882, and merged with Paso Robles in 1934. (Estrella)

Eto Lake- This man-made lake is named for pioneer Japanese-American Tamaji Eto, who owned and farmed the area around the lake. (Morro Bay South)-See photo next page.

Eureka; school district- This district was founded before 1895, and merged with Templeton in 1921. It was named for the Eureka Improvement Company which laid out the townsite of Vasa, where the school was located. The word means 'I found it'. See Vasa.

Excelsior; school district- The district was founded be-

Tamaji and Tame Eto, after whom Eto Lake in Los Osos Valley is named.

fore 1871, and merged into Morro district in 1919. The word means always upward or higher, and was probably chosen to inspire the students.

F air View/Fairview; school district- This district was founded before 1882, and lapsed in 1979.

Fairbank Point- Located just south of Morro Bay, this is named for Dr. and Mrs. Charles Fairbank who lived nearby. [Gudde] (Morro Bay South)

Fern Canyon- There are two canyons bearing this name in the county. The one near Lopez Lake was named for the large ferns growing in the area. (Lopez/ Paso Robles)

Fernandez Creek; spring- Probably named for Hernando Fernandez, an early vaquero on the La Panza ranch. He patented the homestead for the land on which the spring occurs, though the homestead was originally filed by Juana Mesa. (Camatta Ranch/ Pozo)

Fifteen Mile House- Located where Whitley Gardens is today, this roadhouse was named for its location 15 miles east of Paso Robles. Later, when a bridge was built here, it was also known as 15 Mile Bridge, until the Whitley Gardens subdivision was developed. [Bethel] See Whitley Gardens.

Fiscalini Creek- Named for the family of Joseph Fiscalini, who emigrated to this area from Switzerland in 1876. (Cambria)

Fish Creek- Probably named for the fish in the creek. In California place names, fish only accounts for about twenty-five creeks and streams. [Gudde] (Chimney Canyon)

French Camp, about 1880. This view shows the location from the northeast. French Camp is located on the Camatti Ranch. Photo courtesy of Harold Miossi.

Five Willow Spring- See Willow. (Caliente Mountain/ Painted Rock)

Fleming's Forest- A grove of 1200 Monterey Pines planted by John Fleming, State Park Supervisor in 1958, near Morro Bay State Park. [Bailey and Gates]

Franklin Creek- Named for Benjamin H. Franklin, who owned nearly 500 acres along Santa Rosa Creek and 160 acres about three miles from this creek. He was the great grandson of Benjamin Franklin, our first postmaster. (Lime Mountain/ Adelaida)

Franklin; School District- near Cambria, the school may have been named for early resident Benjamin H. Franklin or for the Hester Franklin family. It was founded in 1870, and merged with Cayucos in 1899.

Freeborn Mountain- Named for William Freeborn who moved to the area in 1872, after originally locating in San Luis Obispo in 1869. He was a pioneer in Minnesota before coming to California, and there is a Minnesota county named for him as well. He carried the mail between Santa Margarita and Simmler from 1903-1906. (California Valley)

Freeman Canyon- Likely named for the Rega Dent Freeman family, ranchers in the area. (Estrella)

French Camp- Named for M. Jose Borel and Bartolo Baratie, two French sheepherders who were murdered in 1857 by the Pio Linares/Jack Powers gang on their ranch on San Juan Creek. (La Panza)

French Joe's Canyon- Possibly named for Joe Simmons, a Frenchman near San Miguel

Froom Creek- Named for the Froom family, who owned the ranch for most of the twentieth century through which this creek ran. (SLO/ Pismo Beach)

Garcia Mountain(s)- Named for Julian Garcia who applied for the Rancho San Juan Capistrano, and was denied the grant. He did settle in the area, becoming a prominent rancher. [O'Donovan] Another source claims that the mountain was named for Ynocente Garcia, the "father" of Pozo, who claimed this area originally as a Mexican Land grant and later as a possessory claim. [Pozo Diary] (Caldwell Mesa/ Pozo Summit/ Los Machos Hills/ Santa Margarita Lake)

Garcia Portrero Spring- Near Pozo, this was named for one of the three Garcia families who lived in the area. (Los Machos Hills)

Garden Farms- This was a real estate promotional name for one of E. G. Lewis's subdivisions around Atascadero. It was to be of larger, garden lots. (Santa Margarita)

Garrity Peak- Named for Pat Garrity, who had a homestead near the peak. (San Simeon)

Geneseo; school district- This was a school district and settlement ten miles east of Paso Robles. It was named for Geneseo, Illinois, the hometown of three early families, the Martins, Williams, and John Ernsts. It was a German speaking settlement. The school district was begun with the settlement, and merged with Paso Robles in 1962.

Gibbons; post office- Established on February 15, 1894, this post office was probably named for Lewis Dalton Gibbons who homesteaded 240 acres two miles east of Lime Mountain in 1884. Gibbons served as deputy Coroner for the County in 1892 and died in 1910. The post office was discontinued on September 30, 1909, and mail service was transferred to Adelaida. [MacGillvrey]

Gifford Spring- Named for the Gifford Ranch on which it is located. (Miranda Pine)

Gillis Canyon- Named for the William Gillis family, residents in the area in 1892. The eldest was William Gillis, followed by Napoleon and Leigh Gillis. [White Oral History] (Cholame)

Godfrey; school district- This district was founded in 1898, and merged with the Summit district in 1910. It was named for Henry Godfrey, owner of the Godfrey Ranch.

Gold Hill- Near the Hearst Cholame Ranch headquarters, this hill was the site of placer mining operations as early as the Mission era. [Adams]

Goldtree; SP siding, townsite- Named for the Goldtree family. The Goldtrees were the most successful merchants in San Luis Obispo in the late 1870's and 1880's, and led the commercial move to Higuera Street from Monterey Street when they built the Goldtree Block, today's Hotel Wineman. The Goldtrees gave the property on which this Southern Pacific stop was located. The stop existed as early as 1894, when the SP finally reached SLO. It was through this stop that most of the Chromium ore was shipped from San Luis Obispo County. A townsite was announced at the site of the stop, but never developed. See Chorro. (San Luis Obispo)- See photo next page.

Goodwin; post office, town- This post office started and stopped twice. It was first granted on July 27, 1889, and discontinued on December 15, 1891. It was re-established on February 8, 1892, and discontinued on July 31, 1899. It may have taken its name from the Goodwin ranch, named for its owners, Mr. and Mrs. J. F. Goodwin. (Chimineas Ranch)

Morris Goldtree, whose name is preserved in the Goldtree Siding on the Southern Pacific Railroad above Cal Poly.

Gragg Canyon- (AKA Hidden Canyon) Originally named Cañada de Santa Elena by Father Crespi of the Portolá expedition, or Cañada Angosta by the men of the Portolá expedition, it today carries the name of the George Gragg family, which owned the canyon and lived nearby on the coast. The Graggs were related to Orville Root, postmaster and namesake of the Root Post Office located at Miles Station. See Root, Miles Station. (Pismo Beach)

Granger Spring- Probably named for the Granger family. Twin Granger daughters, Zora and Nora, married twin Truesdale sons, Willis and Ellis, in Shandon in 1895. The double wedding was one of the best known. The joint 50th anniversary celebration was well attended in 1945. [Truesdale] (Cholame)

Granite Ridge- Located northeast of Santa Margarita, this is named for the prevalent stone in the area. (Santa Margarita)

Graves Creek- Possibly named for Groghan Graves, who was born in Kentucky in 1834. He was in the area by 1868. The creek runs through Rocky Gorge. (Atascadero/ Templeton/ Morro Bay North)

Green Valley; canyon- Named for Samuel Green, an early settler. (Cambria/ Cypress Mountain)

Grizzly Bend; lake, spring- These were all named for the California grizzly bear, which was prevalent throughout San Luis Obispo county until the later nineteenth century. (Pebblestone Shut-in/ Creston/ Branch Mountain)

Dwight W. Grover, who founded and named the city which still bears his name.

Grover; City, Beach- post office, town- Named for Dwight W. Grover, the original founder of the community. This was a boom era subdivision, originally founded in 1887 in anticipation of the coming of the Southern Pacific Railroad. When the SP failed to arrive within the year, the subdivision passed from promoter to promoter, until beginning to grow in the late 1930's. It acquired a post office on March 16, 1947, and was incorporated in 1959. Streets in Grover City are named for famous resorts, including Newport, Brighton, Manhattan, and Nice. In 1992, after a public election, the name was changed to Grover Beach by a majority of the voters of the city. (Oceano/ Oceano OE W/ Arroyo Grande NE/ Pismo Beach)

Guadaloupe, Guadalupe- Part of the Rancho Guadaloupe is located in the extreme southwest part of our county. For two years, in the 1850's, all of the rancho was in our county. The rancho, granted to Diego Olivera and Teodoro Arellanes on March 21, 1840. It takes its name from the patron saint of Mexican Catholics, the Virgin of Guadaloupe. (Guadalupe)

Guaya Canyon- This canyon branches off from Newsom Canyon. Its name may derive from aguada, or watery place, referring to the springs in the vicinity, or from guayule, a Mexican plant from which rubber can be derived. (Arroyo Grande NE/ Oceano)

Gull Rock- see Bird Rock

Gypsum Canyon- Named for a gypsum deposit located in the canyon. (Branch Mountain/ Miranda Pine)

Hadley; Pacific Coast Railway (PCR) stop, tower, SP station- This station is shown on the 1918 SP station list. Where the SP crossed the PCR right of way, a tower was manned by the SP 24 hours a day to stop the SP if the PCR was coming. The SP had to build the tower at the insistence of the PCR, since the PCR was built there first.

Halcyon; town, post office, beach - The town of Halcyon was founded by the Temple of the People in 1903. This Theosophical group was founded in Syracuse, New York, in 1898 by Francia LaDue and Dr. William Dower, followers of Helena Blavatsky. The name is a synonym for tranquility or calm. It is derived from the Greek legend of Alcyon, who, with her husband Ceyx, were changed to kingfisher birds after their drowning. Kingfishers were thereafter said to have the power to calm the ocean when they built their nests. Halcyon Beach was an outdoor sanitarium, and an unsuccessful subdivision of part of the dunes south of Oceano by the Temple Home Association (Oceano)

Selected Street Names in Halcyon

Dower- Named for Dr. Dower, cofounder of the community.
Francia- Named for Francia LaDue, cofounder of Halcyon.
Helena- Named for Helena Blavatsky, founder of Theosophy.
Hiawatha- Named for the eastern Indian.
Judge- Named for William Quan Judge.
LaDue- Named for Francia LaDue.
Temple- Named for the Temple of the People.

Hammond Spring- Perhaps named for James T. Hammond, a resident of the area in 1892. He was born in Kentucky in 1829. (Cholame)

Hardie Park- This park in Cayucos is named for Angus M. Hardie, an early resident of the area.

Harford; townsite, canyon, port- This was the name of a failed real estate promotion at the site of Miles, or Castro's, station, the terminus of the Pacific Coast Railway in 1875. The town was laid out, but all that was built was a roadhouse, saloon, and warehouse/station for the San Luis Obispo and Santa Maria Valley Railroad, later known as the Pacific Coast Railway. It was named for John Harford, one of its developers, and founder of the railroad. The canyon and port were named for the same man. See Port Harford/Port San Luis. (Pismo Beach/ Port San Luis)

Harlech Castle Rock- This rock is named for the bark *Harlech Castle* which ran aground here on August 30, 1869. (Piedras Blancas)

Harmony; town, post office, school district, valley- The valley received the name Harmony when peace prevailed in the 1860's after a period of local fighting. When the post office for the new town was applied for, M. G. Salmina, of the Harmony Creamery, suggested the name Harmony in 1915. The post office was granted on April 20, 1915, and is still in operation at the time of this writing. The school district was begun in 1875, and merged with Cambria in 1930. (Cambria)

Harris Canyon- This canyon, on the Monterey - San Luis Obispo County border is named for Ethelbert Harris. It is referred to as being near Cantinas School in the north county and the site of the Birdhaven School in an oral history done with Clyde and Velma Dayton in 1965.

Hathway Avenue; SP station- This station was listed in the 1894 and 1899 SP station listings, and was located in San Luis Obispo just north of the Ramona Hotel. It was named for the Hathway family who owned land in the area.

Hathway Place- Probably named for "Bun" Hathway, an old resident and well known cowboy and rancher in the area. (Caldwell Mesa)

Havel; SP station- This station is listed in 1899 SP station list, and shown as 1 mile south of the Atascadero station in 1918.

Hawaiian Hot Springs- Commercial name for the Ontario Hot Springs from 1969 until 1971. Chosen for tourist potential, it did not last. (Pismo Beach)

Hazard Canyon- This canyon was named for Robert Hazard, on whose ranch it was located. It is now part of the Moñtana de Oro State Park. (Morro Bay South/ Morro Bay South OE W)

Hazel Station- See Dove

Hearst Castle - See La Cuesta Encantada

Henry; SP station- This station was shown as four miles south of Templeton in the 1918 SP station listing. It was named for J. H. Henry, the owner of the Asuncion ranch when the railroad came through in 1888. (Atascadero)

Henry's Forks- On the Asuncion ranch, this referred to the owner of the ranch, J. H. Henry.

Hesperian School District- This was the original name for the Cambria School district, and was begun in 1868.

Hidden Valley; hot springs- Hidden Valley was the name for the small valley which connects with the Avila Valley near the Ontario Hot Springs. It was destroyed by the building of the new Ontario grade on Highway 101 in the late 1950's. The Ontario Hot Springs was known by this name for a few years. (Pismo Beach)

The Hollister Adobe about 1880. Hollister Peak is named for the family, and was located on their ranch.

Highland; school district- This district began about 1888, and merged with Huer Huero in 1942.

Hog Canyon- This canyon was earlier known as Echo Canyon. It may have been named for hog ranching in the area, or for wild hogs, which were numerous in the area. (Ranchito Canyon/ Estrella)

Hollister Peak- Originally called Cerro Alto, or high peak, this peak was renamed in 1884 by the Coast Survey for the Hollister family which owned the ranch at the base of the peak. Other names for this peak have included Quintana, Morro Twin, and Santa Rosita. [Gudde] (Morro Bay South) - See photo previous page.

Home; school district- This school was originally located in Dr. Eleutheros Clark's home, for which it was named. Before this, the school had been known as the Log School, and had met in a rough hewn log house. [Hamilton] The district was founded in 1874, and suspended in 1938.

Hope; school district- This district was begun in 1870, and merged with the Banning district in 1943.

Hopper Canyon- Perhaps named for William Hopper, a registered voter in San Miguel in 1871. (Cholame)

Horse Mesa, canyon- Horses were the primary means of transportation in early Spanish and American California. During the American period, many places were named for the horse. There are over 500 such placenames in California. [Gudde] (Santa Margarita Lake/ New Cuyama/ Wells Ranch)

Hospital Lake- One of the dune lakes, this was probably named for the outdoor sanitarium run by the Halcyon Theosophical colony. (Oceano)

Hot Springs; post office- An early name for the Paso Robles Hot Springs, this was the name of the post office at the site from June 14, 1867 until November 21, 1867, and again from February 7, 1868 until May 2, 1870. This was before the founding of the town of Paso Robles, though the hot springs were a stage stop. The hot springs were first recorded by Father Font in 1776. See Paso de Robles.

Huasna; valley, landgrant, town, creek, post office, school district- This is a Chumash word whose meaning is unknown. A rancheria, or native American village, was shown on the diseño of the Rancho Arroyo Grande in 1842 as Guasna. It was later applied to the Rancho Huasna landgrant given to Isaac Sparks on December 8, 1843, and from there was eventually applied to the town, post office and school district. The post office was in operation, according to post office records, from October 19, 1899 to September 15, 1910, though postmarks are known as late as 1912. The school district was founded before 1882. A tale associated with the name is that Huasna was the name of the favorite daughter of a Tulare chief, who used the area for a summer encampment. An early example of this particular piece of folklore can be found in the San Luis Obispo Tribune in 1892. (Nipomo/ Caldwell Mesa/ Huasna Peak/ Tar Spring Ridge)

Hubbard Hill- Probably named for Aristarchus Francis Hubbard, an early settler who established a mill on the

Aristarchus F. Hubbard, blacksmith, inventor, promoter and mill operator, whose name is commemorated in Hubbard Hill.

Carrisa Plain. The mill used stones from the Bonilla La Cuesta Mill, which were originally from France. The stones were later purchased by Mrs. Annie Lowe and returned to the Cuesta area. The remnants of one is now in the County Historical Museum. Hubbard was also noted for inventing an all metal dirigible, which was never built because of his death in 1903. (California Valley)

Huerhuero/Huer Huero; landgrant, creek, school district- The school district was begun before 1882, and was merged with Creston in 1924. It was named for a site called Huerguero, according to Gudde, who records a reference in the Legislative Records of the Archivo de California, transcripts of which are in the Bancroft Library. (Creston/ Santa Margarita/ Wilson Corner/ Shedd Canyon)

Huerta de Romualdo; landgrant- At the base of Cerro Romualdo, this translates from the Spanish into the kitchen garden of Romualdo. It was named for its grantee, the only Indian to be given a landgrant in San Luis Obispo County. Romualdo received the land in 1842, but soon lost it to John Wilson who owned the huge Cañada de Los Osos y Pecho y Islay Rancho next to it. (SLO)

Huff's Hole; creek, flat- Named for a sheepherder who had a cabin near the creek. (Tar Spring Ridge/ Santa Margarita Lake)

Hughes Canyon; spring- Perhaps named for "Dr." Hughes, the doctor in Shandon about the turn of the century. [Truesdale] (Camatta Canyon/ Holland Canyon)

Huntington Beach- That part of the beach which borders Grover Beach was renamed Huntington Beach during the early 1890's, when new promoters tried to sell lots in the townsite of Grover. Neither the sales promotion, nor the renaming of the beach, were successful.

I ndependence; school district- This district was begun in 1910, and merged with the Corral de Piedra and East Santa Fe districts to form the Los Ranchos school in 1959. It was formed close to two existing districts and was named for the independent spirit of the families whose children were to attend the school. They wanted their own school, and they had it. (Arroyo Grande NE)

Indian Knob- This is the highest point at 884 feet in the range which separates the San Luis Creek and Price Canyon watersheds. It was probably named for its proximity to Chief Buchon's village. [Miossi] (Pismo Beach)

Irish Hills; school district- This area was named for a number of Irish families who settled here in the nineteenth century. These included the McEntee, McArdle, McHenry, Coll and Connolly families. The school district started in 1912 and merged with the Laguna district in 1943. (Port San Luis/ Pismo Beach/ San Luis Obispo/ Morro Beach)

Iron Springs; school district- This school district near Creston was begun about 1886, and was merged with the Creston Union district in 1924. It was named for a natural spring high in iron which was in the area. There is also an Iron Spring in the Branch Mountain area of the south county. (Branch Mountain/ Santa Margarita)

Islay Hill; creek- This term is taken from the Salinan word Yslay or Slay, meaning wild cherry or chokecherry. The first use of the term is in Fages' 1775 description of California. It was first applied to the Pecho y Islay landgrant, as Islay Creek was the northernmost boundary of the grant. Islay Hill is inland from San Luis Obispo, and is one of the range of hills which stretch from the Davidson Seamount and Morro Rock to Islay Hill. (Arroyo Grande NE/ Morro Bay South)

The Klau Mine, in Adelaida district, which gave its name to the Klau Post Office.

J ack Canyon- Probably named for the Jack family of San Luis Obispo, who owned the Cholame Ranch. (Orchard Peak)

Jack Creek; mountain- Named for Miss Christine Jack, a native of Scotland who operated a ranch in the area in the late 1800's. She discovered and worked the Bonnie Doon Quicksilver Mine. (York Mountain/ Cypress Mountain)

Jack Lake- This Dune lake was perhaps named for Robert E. Jack, because of his involvement with the founding of Oceano. (Oceano)

Jespersen Spring- Probably named for Chris H. Jesperson, resident of this area in 1892. (Cholame)

Josephine; post office, mine, school district- The Josephine post office was located at and took its name from the Josephine quicksilver mine. The post office was established on March 28, 1873 and discontinued on March 16, 1877. It was re-established on September 18, 1877, and discontinued for a final time on February 5, 1883. The school district was founded before 1882, and was merged into the Ascension district in 1931. The mine was named for the first white child born in the area.

Juhl; post office- This post office was established on May 28, 1915. It was named for the first postmaster, George H. Juhl. It was rescinded on October 1, 1915, and was never put into operation. It was located on the Santa Rita Rancho, about nine miles from Cayucos.

Kessler Onyx Mine- Located off Hi Mountain Road, this mine was named for the Kessler Brothers of San Francisco, who developed the property.

**Keyes Canyon; ** school district- This canyon name shows on the 1874 County Map. The only Keyes I have located in the county previous to this is James Keyes, who had $5,150 in assessed property in 1860. No Keyes are listed as registered voters in 1867 or 1871. The school district was founded about 1890, and merged with Pleasant Valley in 1920. (Ranchito Canyon/ Estrella/ Cholame Hills)

Kiler Canyon- Perhaps named for Samuel Harrison Kiler, resident in the Paso Robles voting district in 1892. (Templeton)

**Klau; ** post office, mine- This post office takes its name from the nearby Klau quicksilver mine, which was named for its owner Karl Klau. The Klau had earlier been known as the Sunderland, before its purchase by Klau. It was established on July 9, 1901 and discontinued on October 31, 1924. See Sunderland. (Lime Mountain) - See Photo page 73.

William Randolph Hearst's La Cuesta Encantada, the enchanted hill, under construction. Today the site is better known as Hearst's Castle.

La Cuesta Encantada- This was the name given by William Randolph Hearst in 1924 to the hill on which he built his "castle." It means the enchanted hill in Spanish. He never referred to the building as a castle, preferring instead the term La Casa Grande, or the grand house. The hill was originally called Camp Hill by the Hearst family, as it was the site of the old family campground. (San Simeon)

La Grande Beach- This failed townsite was laid out on the Oceano Dunes. Its name, in Spanish, means the grand beach, and was a real estate promotional name. Now part of the Pismo Dunes State Park.

La Panza, Lapanza; post office, range, canyon, camp, summit- The post office took its name from the La Panza mine, according to the recollections of Birma Still MacLean in 1943. The term refers to the paunch of a beef used to catch bears. The paunch would be hung in a tree at a height that only bears could reach, and poisoned by the Chumash and Salinan Indians, to slow a bear until it could be killed. The name appears to have first been used for this area in 1828, when it was referred to as Paraje La Panza, or place of the paunch, by Sebastian Rodriguez. The post office was established on November 4, 1879, as one word and was changed to two words in 1905. It was discontinued on June 15, 1908, but re-established on April 29, 1911. It was finally discontinued April 20, 1935. The school district was formed in 1883, and merged with Pozo in 1930. (La Panza)

La Playa, Laplaya; post office- This post office was established on May 17, 1876. The first postmaster, David

P. Mallagh, was running the People's Wharf at Avila. The name was changed to two words on June 12, 1876, and discontinued on December 27, 1878. It was probably discontinued because of the destruction of the People's Wharf in a bad storm in January 1878. The words are Spanish for the beach, and reflect the site.

Laguna; landgrant, lake, school district- This is the Spanish word for lake, and is one of the redundant names in our county, Laguna Lake being Lake Lake. The school district was founded before 1882. (San Luis Obispo)

Lake Ysabel- Man-made lake near Paso Robles formed by a small dam on Santa Ysabel creek, known as Arroyo de Santa Ysabel in 1797.

A circa 1900 view of Laguna Lake, or lake lake. This is one of the instances where local Spanish placenames have been translated in the modern name.

William Leffingwell, namesake and proprietor of Leffingwell's Landing.

Lang's Canyon- This canyon near San Miguel is named for the Lang family which settled here. [McIntosh]

Las Pilitas- In common usage, this was a Spanish term meaning small bowls or basins, according to research done by Col. and Mrs. Albert Ferguson of the Las Pilitas Ranch. [Dart] (Lopez Mountain/ Santa Margarita Lake)

Las Tablas; canyon, creek, post office, school district- In Spanish, this means the boards, slabs, or tables, referring to wood. This district was formed in 1879, and transferred to the Sunderland district in 1900. (Lime Mountain/ Cypress Mountain/ Adelaida)

Las Yeguas- See Yeguas.

Leffingwell Creek; landing- Named for William Leffingwell and his family, the private wharf was just north of Cambria and operated in the late nineteenth century. (Cambria)

Lettuce Lake- This Dune lake was probably named for the large amount of lettuce grown in the area. (Oceano)

Lime Mountain- This was named for the limestone deposit located here. (Lime Mountain)

Lincoln; school district- This district was started in 1881, and merged with the Sunderland district in 1948 to form the Adelaida district. Probably named for Abraham Lincoln.

Lingo Canyon- Probably named for George Lingo, early resident of Pozo. (Pozo Summit)

Linne; town, post office, school district- This was a Swedish settlement in the north county which was named in honor of Karl von Linne, the Swedish naturalist and botanist. Its post office was established on January 22, 1889 and discontinued on November 14, 1925. The school district was founded about 1891, and merged with Geneseo in 1924. (Creston)

Lion Rock- Named either for the large number of sea lions which congregate on it, or its resemblance to a sea lion, this rock lies off Diablo Cove on the Pecho Coast. During the Mexican era, the rock was known as El Lobo, or the wolf, referring to sea lions. [Gudde] (Port San Luis)

Little Burnett Creek- See Burnett Peak. (Pebblestone Shut-in/ Bryson/ Burnett Peak)

Little Cayucos Creek- See Cayucos. (Cayucos)

Little Creek- Little is often used to designate places which resemble larger sites nearby. [Gudde]

Little Morro Creek- See Morro. (Morro Bay North)

Little Oso Flaco Lake- This is a small dune lake near Oso Flaco Lake, and is named for it. (Oceano)

Lodge Hill- Named for the Cambria Pines Lodge, located on the hill. Earlier known as Bachelor's Hill, because the only resident on the hill was a bachelor. [Tyson]

Logan; PCR stop- This Pacific Coast Railway stop was located just north of Corbett Canyon. I have not found the origin of the name.

Logan Ridge; creek- between Branch Creek and Cuyama River. Perhaps named for John Hulet Logan, resident of the Alamo Creek area and registered voter in the Huasna area in 1892. (Chimney Canyon/ Los Machos Hills)

Loma Pelona- In Spanish, this means bald hill. This was often applied to hills or mountains with few trees on the summit. (Nipomo)

Loma Pilon; school district- Probably misnamed for Loma Pelona which was near the district location, the school district was founded in 1898 and merged with Nipomo and Los Berros in 1918.

Lone Black Rock- This rock, off the Port San Luis Lighthouse, is named for its color. (Port San Luis)

Lone Rock- This was named for the lack of any other rocks in close proximity. (Pismo)

Lone Tree Hill- Named for the single tree which grew at the top of this hill. This was an early mariner's landmark. (San Simeon)

Long Canyon; valley, cave, ridge- There are at least three Long Canyons in San Luis Obispo County, one near Huasna, one near the Camatta Ranch, and one near Cambria, as well as a Long Valley near Atascadero. The name probably relates in each case to its length. (Tar Spring Ridge/ Caldwell Mesa/ Huasna Peak/ Holland Canyon/ La Panza Ranch/ Camatta Ranch/ Atascadero/ Templeton/ Orchard Peak/ Branch Mountain)

Lopez; lake, mountain, canyon, dam, school district- Called Cañada del Trigo from Mission times to the 1870's for the wheat which was grown here, this area is now named for Juan and Jesus Lopez, who homesteaded in the canyon. Trigo, meaning wheat in Spanish, referred to an attempt by the Mission to grow wheat in the canyon, which was abandoned because of too many deer eating the wheat. [Ditmas] The school district was created in 1902, and merged with Santa Manuela in 1927. (Tar Spring Ridge/ Santa Margarita Lake/ Lopez Mountain)

Los Berros; creek, canyon, town, post office, school district-Named for Los Berros creek. See Berros. (Oceano/ Nipomo)

Los Osos; valley, town, post office, school district- Originally called La Cañada de Los Osos, the valley which runs from San Luis Obispo to the coast at Los Osos/ Baywood Park was named by the men of the Portolá expedition on September 7, 1869. The name refers to the large number of California grizzly bears encountered in the valley. Father Juan Crespi named the valley La Natividad de Nuestra Señora, a name which was not popularly utilized. Pedro Fages, then governor of California, remembered the number of bears, and lead a hunting expedition to the valley three years later. The success of this expedition caused Father Junipero Serra to found Mission San Luis Obispo. The school district was formed in 1872, and merged with the Laguna district in 1958. (San Luis Obispo/ Morro Bay North)

Los Padres; post office, National Forest- The national forest was named in 1938 by then-President Franklin Roosevelt. It was chosen to honor the Franciscan Missionaries. It refers to the forest which was formed when the San Luis Obispo (1906), Santa Barbara (1908), and other National Forests were combined. The post office of this name was located at the California Men's Colony, a State Prison located west of San Luis Obispo on Highway 1. It was a branch of the San Luis Obispo Post Office, and operated from November 1, 1956 until April 30, 1966. (Lopez Mountain/ Ballinger Canyon/ Santiago Canyon/ Eagle Rest Peak/ Pleito Hills/ Cuyama Peak)

Los Pelados; peak- Located between Machesna and Branch mountains, this means the bare or naked, or the penniless or broke, in colloquial spoken Spanish. (Los Machos Hills)

Lowe Hill- Now part of Cal Poly's ranch land, this was

named for early rancher and owner Dawson Lowe. (San Luis Obispo)

Lowe's Canyon- This canyon, near San Miguel, is named for Frank Lowe and his family. Lowe settled here in 1865 after moving from Healdsburg, California. This canyon was originally known as San Jacinto (St. Hyacinth) Canyon. (Paso Robles/ San Miguel/ Ranchito Canyon/ Stockdale)

Lynch; post office, canyon- Named for James Lynch, who settled here in 1859. He came to California as part of Stevenson's regiment and later married Alice Kennedy, a schoolteacher in San Francisco, before moving to his ranch called Tierra Redonda. Alice Kennedy Lynch was the first postmaster of this ranch post office, which ran from April 23, 1894 to December 31, 1912.

MacDonald Canyon- Perhaps named for Archibald McDonald, resident and registered voter of the Estrella area in 1892. This canyon is located south of Shandon.

Machesna/McChesney Mountain; portrero, spring, trail, wilderness area- Named for the McChesney family. (La Panza)

Maggetti Flats- This is named for the owner of a nearby ranch. (Santa Margarita Lake)

Mahoney Canyon; grove- Located near San Miguel, this was named for pioneer James Mahoney. He arrived in San Miguel before 1870, and later served as County Recorder. (San Miguel)

Mallagh Landing- See Cave Landing (Pismo Beach)

Mammoth Rock; rock, school district- The school district takes its name from this rock outcropping at the head of the Santa Rosa Valley. The name refers to the size and prominence of the outcropping. The district was founded in 1868 and merged with Cambria in 1945. (Cypress Mountain)

Manzanita Canyon- Named for the prevalent manzanita plants in the area. (Cholame Hills/ Shandon)

Maple; school district- This district was formed about 1900, and merged with the Independence district in 1915.

Mariana Grade; canyon, creek- The grade, canyon and

spring are located between Pozo and La Panza. (Pozo Summit)

Marmolejo Creek- In Spanish this would mean little marble creek. (Pebblestone Shut-in)

Marre Island- A small island which formerly existed at the Avila end of San Luis Creek. Named for Luigi Marre, this island was obliterated when the creek was straightened and the channel surrounding the island filled in.

Martinez Canyon- This was named for Chico Martinez, a well respected mustang runner. [Gudde] (La Panza)

Maxwellton; townsite- In 1894, Lynferd Maxwell laid out a new community in the Edna Valley which he named for himself. There had been a post office named Edna at the site since 1887, and Maxwellton never caught on for the new community. See Edna.

McChesney Canyon- See Machesna Mountain. (La Panza)

McChesney Field- Official name of the San Luis Obispo Airport, it honors Leroy McChesney, an Edna Valley dairy owner and aviator.

McClure's/McClure Valley- Named for McClure, shown as resident here on an 1874 County map.

McDonald Canyon- Probably named for Captain McDonald, early owner of much of the Carrisa Plain. (Camatta Canyon)

McKay; SP station- This was the junction of the Stone Canyon Railway and the Southern Pacific, north of San Miguel. It was named for Hood McKay, owner of the Stone Canyon Coal Mine. The Stone Canyon Pacific Railroad was a short line serving a coal mining operation in Stone Canyon in southern Monterey County. It is listed as an A class freight station in the 1914 SP station listing. The station was closed when the mine was closed. See Chancellor. [Adams] (San Miguel)

McMillan Canyon- Originally called New Brunswick Canyon, for the city where James McMillan grew up, the name was later changed to McMillan Canyon, after him and his family. They moved here in 1885. (Cholame Valley/ Shandon/ Cholame)

Mehlschau Creek- This is named for the Mehlschau family, early residents of Nipomo. (Nipomo)

Mercury; School district- This extremely short lived district was formed in 1918, and merged with the Mammoth Rock district in 1921. It was named for the large amounts of mercury mined in the area.

Middle Canyon; ridge- There are two canyons and one ridge by this name in the county. They are all named for their location. (Cholame Hills/ Pebblestone Shut-in/ New Cuyama/ Wells Ranch)

Miles Station; PCR station- This station was named for Elbridge Miles, who operated the freight warehouse. [PR Cent.] The site was earlier known as Castro's Station. The warehouse was also the site of the Root Post Office, and the failed townsites of Harford and Monte. See also Castro's Station, Root, Harford, and Monte. (Pismo Beach)

Mill Creek- Located 30 miles north of San Simeon, this creek was named for a sawmill located along the creek. [Thorndyke]

Mine Hill- There are actually two mine hills in the county. One, also known as Righetti Hill, for the family which

The original Miles Station in the Avila Valley, showing the Pacific Coast Railway tracks in the foreground. In addition to the Miles name, this was the site of the Root Post Office, and the townsites of Harford and Monte, and was near the townsite of Ynocenta.

owned the ranch which surrounded the hill, is located next to Islay Hill in the City limits of San Luis Obispo. It gets the name from an early chromium mining operation worked by Pierre Dallidet which is still visible on the side of the hill. The other Mine Hill is located just south west of San Luis Obispo on the old Froom Ranch, and takes its name from a Chromium Mine on the hill. (Pismo Beach/ Arroyo Grande NE)

Minneola- Though this post office is listed in official Post Office records as being in San Luis Obispo County, it never was. This was actually in San Bernadino county, and was named for Minnie Dieterle, wife of one of the promoters of the townsite. [Salley]

Mission; school district- This was the name for the first school district in San Luis Obispo County. The first school was in Mission San Luis Obispo, and when a new school building was built, it was called the Mission School. The district took its name from this.

Montaña de Oro; ranch, state park- This was the northern 4,500 acres of the Spooner Ranch, and was purchased by Irene Starkey McAllister in 1954. She renamed this area. There are two versions of the renaming; one that it was in tribute to her husband being from Montana, or two, because of the bush monkey flowers and mustard in bloom on Valencia Peak. I would be more inclined to accept the latter. The State Park system purchased the property in 1965. [Miossi] (Morro Bay South/ Port San Luis/ Port San Luis OE W/ Morro Bay South OE W)

Monte- This was another of the many failed real estate

promotions which exist in our county. It was at the site of Miles Station on the Pacific Coast Railway, and was promoted by Schwartz, Beebee and Company. It was named for the type of landscape in the area, monte in Spanish meaning thicket or woods.

Moonstone Beach- Named for the large number of moonstones found on this beach north of Cambria.

Morales Canyon- Named for Julio Morales, a nineteenth century Mexican bandit who later ranched in the area. [O'Donovan] (Caliente Mountain)

Moretti Canyon- Located on the Corral de Piedra, this is named for Giacoma Moretti, an early landowner. [County Road File 204]

Morro/ Morro Bay; rock, bay, landgrant, creek, plaza, school district- This is one of those names for which there are many explanations. Local historian and writer Dan Krieger has written that the rock was named by Cabrillo in 1542, and refers to the shape of a Moor's turban. It was originally spelled with one r, the second being added later. The term morro with two r's is Spanish for a high land mass above a harbor capable of holding fortifications. The town received its post office on December 14, 1870. Bay was added on November 16, 1923 for promotional reasons. The Moro Rancho was granted to Martin Olivera on April 27, 1842, and was patented to James McKinley, after being combined with Vicente Feliz's Cayucos landgrant, on January 19, 1878.

Morro Rock, about 1910.

Mount Lowe- This prominent hill in Cuesta Canyon is named for the Jackson Lowe family, early settlers in this area. [Miossi] (Lopez Mountain)

Mountain View; school district- Named for the geography of the area, this district was formed before 1882, and merged with the Banning district in 1948.

Moy Mell- This was a settlement in the sand dunes south of Oceano. Founded by Gavin Arthur, grandson of President Chester A. Arthur, it was named by mystic and Celtic scholar Ella Young after visiting there. The name means pasture of honey.

Mud Lake- One of the dune lakes, this is named for its color. (Oceano)

Murray Hill- Name adopted for the hill in behind the County Hospital in 1887. Name was in honor of Walter Murray, pioneer citizen and founder of the San Luis

Obispo Tribune. (Daily Republic, 5-23-1887)

Musick; post office- Named for Lanson Trigg Musick, an early settler in the area. Abrum Hasbrouck bought Musick's homestead when he was building his St. Remy ranch, and when he applied for a post office for the area, he named it for the early settler. The post office operated from December 14, 1880 until March 15, 1921.

Walter Murray, whose name is remembered in Murray Hill and Murray Street in San Luis Obispo.

Nacimiento; river, canyon, reservoir, school district, ranch, Southern Pacific stop- This name was applied to the river by Anza, through a misunderstanding of notes from the Portolá expedition. In Crespi's narrative of the expedition, he noted the Indians in the area said that the source, nacimiento, of the river was near where they were camped. Anza apparently felt that the river was named for the Nativity of Christ, Nacimiento, and so referred to the river. This error ended up being formalized as the name of the river, for which the rest were named. [Gudde] A more colorful explanation of the name came from Mariano Vallejo, who wrote that his father, Ignacio Vallejo, traveled through our county in 1772, and came upon a lady about to give birth with no one but her husband to assist. He helped with the birth, and a girl was born. He thereupon asked for the girl's hand in marriage when she should be old enough, and the parents consented, and the happy couple was married 14 years later. Vallejo was known for his stories, and this one is related here for humor, not for accuracy. [Daily Republic, 1-28-1890] A short lived school district by this name existed from 1917 until 1919. The SP stop is shown as early as the 1899 SP station listing. (Bradley/ Tierra Redonda Mountain/ Lime Mountain/ Pebblestone Shut-in/ Bryson/ Burnett Peak)

Nacitone- Soil Conservation District in northern San Luis Obispo County, the name comes from Nacimiento and San Antonio, the two watersheds the district covers. [Dayton]

Navajo; creek, canyon, range, camp, grade, trail- The creek was named for a Navajo woman traveling with sheepherders to French Camp, according to Robert Lewis, owner of the Navajo Ranch. (Camatta Ranch/ Pozo Summit/ La Panza Ranch)

Nelson Canyon- This is the canyon Froom Creek runs through. It is named for Ludwick Nelson, an early owner of the ranch. (San Luis Obispo/ Pismo Beach)

New; school district- This district was formed about 1884, and merged with Santa Margarita. The name refers to it being a new district.

New Era; School District- This district was formed in 1870, and was located north of San Simeon. It is probably named for the New Era Mine.

Newsom; springs, ridge, canyon, school district- This hot springs was named and developed by David F. Newsom. He was a son-in-law of Francis Ziba Branch, to whom the area belonged, and was given the hot springs as a wedding gift. This was a noted resort during the late nineteenth and early twentieth century. The area also gave its name to a school district. The Newsom School District was formed in 1885 and merged with Arroyo Grande in 1901. (Oceano/ Nipomo/ Arroyo Grande NE)

Nipomo, Nipoma; landgrant, town, post office, hill, mesa, creek, valley, school district- This was a Chumash village name. According to Juan Francisco Dana's reminiscences, the local Chumash said the word meant place at the foot of the hill. It should be spelled with a final o, but on at least one cancellation device, an a was used. The landgrant, one of the first three granted in San Luis Obispo County, was given April 6, 1837. The earliest mention of the name is in the records of Mission La Purisima Conception, between 1799 and 1822. The school district was formed in 1883. (Nipomo)

Nova; SP station- This station is four miles south of the Cuesta summit and was established in 1894.

Oak, Oaks- This is a part of many place names in our county. The large number of beautiful oak trees made this a popular name, as in the school districts of Oak Dale (pre 1895 to post 1937), Oak Flat (pre 1895 to 1934), Oak Grove (pre 1895 to 1903), and Oak Park (pre 1895 to post 1937), and the Oak Knoll creek. The Fair Oaks subdivision, a real estate development name, is now part of Arroyo Grande. It had a branch post office named Oaks, which operated from June 1, 1949 until September 7, 1962. The name of Fair Oaks is now remembered only in a few businesses on Grand Avenue near Halcyon in Arroyo Grande and in Fair Oaks Boulevard in the same area. There was also a Fair Oaks Ranch in the Adelaida area, which is not related to the Arroyo Grande area. Other oak tree related placenames include Blue Oak and Live Oak Springs, and Black Oak Mountain.

Oceano about 1895, showing the Pacific Ocean for which it was named.

Oats Peak- Located near Moñtana de Oro, this is probably named for the wild oats in the area.

Oat Springs- Located along the Godfrey Road near the Godfrey Ranch. The road is known today as Nacimiento Lake Drive. It was named for the oats in the area.

Ocean Beach Spur; SP spur track south of Oceano- listed in 1899 SP station listing, this spur track ran towards the beach from just south of Oceano station. It was a descriptive name.

Oceanic Creek- One of the three north forks of the Santa Rosa Creek, this one is named for the Oceanic Quicksilver Mine.

Oceano; town, post office, school district- This community was founded in 1893, and was originally to be called Deltina. Within a few weeks the name was changed to La Bolsa, and then to Oceano, Spanish for ocean. It was a real estate name, to capitalize on its location. The school district was formed about 1910. (Oceano)

Oil Wells- See Sycamore Hot Springs.

Oilport; post office- This was the site of an oil refinery, funded with British investment funds and built by the California Petroleum Refineries, Ltd. The refinery operated for only two weeks in November and December of 1907. There was a post office on the site from March 27, 1907 until February 29, 1908. The area is known today as Sunset Palisades, a real estate promotional name from the early 1960's. See photo next page.

Oil Refinery, Oilport near San Luis Obispo, Cal.

Oilport, today's Sunset Palisades, took its name from the oil refinery which was built there in 1907. It operated for only two weeks before the loss of its wharf in a storm led to its permanent closure.

Old Creek; settlement, creek, canyon, post office- This is an English translation of the name of the creek as shown on the San Luis Obispo to Rosaville road map of 1870. On that map, the creek is named Arroyo Viejo. (Cayucos/ Morro Bay North/ York Mountain)

Olmstead; school district- Named in honor of Rufus Olmsted, who homesteaded in Green Valley in 1866. He died in 1867, the year before the district's founding. The name was misspelled by the county after its founding, as it is listed as "Olmsted" as late as 1871. [Trib. 12-1870/ Hamilton]

Ontario; house, grade, hot springs- This grade, located between the road to Avila and Sunset Palisades on Highway 101 was originally named for the Ontario House, located on the property of Hermann Budan. Budan had helped locate the Ontario Mine in the Comstock Load, and later sold it to George Hearst. His daughter drilled for oil on the property after inheriting it, and found hot water instead, which led to the creation of the Ontario Hot Springs. This resort has also been known as the Hidden Valley Hot Springs and the Plunge, and today is called the Avila Hot Springs. (Pismo Beach)

Orange; School District- This district was formed about 1889, and merged with the Cholame district in 1899.

Orcutt Knob- Named for J. H. Orcutt who had a ranch east of San Luis Obispo. (Arroyo Grande NE)

Oro Fino Canyon- This is Spanish for fine gold. (Bradley)

Orr's Station- Stagecoach stop shown on the Circa 1880 map of the county road from San Miguel to Cholame, Road #26. It was located near Sheid Canyon.

Ortega Canyon- Near McMillan canyon, this may have been named for Victor Ortega, a vaquero registered to vote in Shandon in 1892. (Shandon/ Cholame)

Oso Creek- In Spanish, this means bear creek. (Caldwell Mesa)

Oso Flaco; lake, creek, school district- This southernmost of the "dune lakes" of the south county was named for a thin bear, or oso flaco, killed and eaten on September 3, 1769, by members of the Portolá expedition. The bear was noted for its savory meat and the fact that it weighed about

375 pounds. The next day 11 of the soldiers complained of leg or stomach problems, probably because the bear had been poisoned by the Chumash living in the area to eventually slow it down enough to kill it. Father Crespi named the lake, The Lake of the Holy Martyrs, San Juan de Perucia and San Pedro de Sacro Terrato. Somehow, I think Oso Flaco is easier to remember. The school district was formed about 1875, and merged with the Guadalupe school district in 1929. (Oceano/ Oceano OE W/ Guadalupe)

Owl/Owlville- This was a Southern Pacific construction camp located on the Cuesta Ranch. It was probably located here because of a nearby spring. It is not listed as an active siding after the completion of the railroad into San Luis Obispo, and was used during construction to house black construction workers outside San Luis Obispo. The siding name is not found in published SP listings. [Krieger/Miossi]

Pacific; school district- This school district in San Simeon was formed before 1882, and is named for the Pacific Ocean.

Padrones Canyon; spring- The spring is shown with this name on the 1874 County Map. Padrone means indulgent parent or pattern in Spanish. The canyon probably takes its name from the spring. (Wells Ranch/ New Cuyama/ Elkhorn Hills)

Painted Rock; Chumash pictograph site, post office- This site on the Carrisa Plain was noted for its pictographs starting in the mid nineteenth century. It was first photographed in 1876 by local photographer R.R.R. Holmes, and has been all but destroyed by visitors. The spectacular nature of the site has led to its being known throughout the region. (Painted Rock)

Palmer Flats- May be named for M.E. Palmer, an early county surveyor who did road surveying in the area. (Cambria)

Palo Prieto; canyon, pass, post office- In Spanish, this means dark tree. (Orchard Peak/ Cholame/ Holland Canyon)

Paloma Creek; SP siding- Paloma means pigeon or dove in Spanish. Paloma siding on the Southern Pacific was later renamed Dove, and was near the State Hospital in Atascadero. See Dove. (Atascadero)

Park Hill School District- This district was formed before 1895, and merged into Santa Margarita in 1943.

Paso Robles, Paso de Robles; land grant, town, post office, school district- In Spanish, Paso de Robles means pass of the oaks. The oak trees in this area were noted by Font in 1776, and the earliest recorded mention of the name as a rancho is in 1828. The hot springs here were utilized by the Salinan Indians before the coming of the missionaries, and were an early claim to fame during the American period. The post office of this name was established on May 2, 1870. See also Hot Springs. (Paso Robles/ Templeton)

Selected Street Names in Paso Robles

Blackburn- Named for the Blackburn brothers.
Creston- Named for the town of Creston.
James- Named for Drury James.
Park- Named because it is bisected by the City Park.
Riverside- Named for its proximity to the Salinas River.
Spring- Named for the hot springs which led to the development of the city.
Union- Named for the settlement of Union.

Peachy Canyon- This canyon was named for A. C. Peachy, an early president of the Oceanic Mine. (Adelaida)

Pebblestone Shut-in- A shut-in is a geological formation, and pebblestone refers to the number of small pebbles on the beach at this location. (Pebblestone Shut-in)

Pecho; coast, peak, creek, school district, hot spring, landgrant, rock- This is a Spanish term meaning a woman's breast. It is first noted as being applied in our county on the diseño of the San Miguelito landgrant where the northern boundary of the landgrant is the Arroyo del Pecho. Pecho Creek was later the southern boundary of the Pecho y Islay landgrant, given to Francisco Padilla on April 27, 1843. This was later combined with the Cañada de Los Osos to be granted as the Rancho Cañada de Los Osos y Pecho y Islay, to John Wilson and James Scott on September 24, 1845. The school district was formed before 1895, and merged into Irish Hills in 1938. (Port San Luis)

Pedro Garcia Creek- See Pennington Creek.

Pennington Creek- Named for John Pennington, an early resident of the Chorro Valley. He was a native of Illinois, born in 1819. Pennington was also the founder of the Daily Republic newspaper. On the 1870 map of the SLO - Cambria road, this creek is shown as Pedro Garcia Creek. [Stechman] (San Luis Obispo/ Morro Bay South)

People's Wharf- Wharf built at Avila in 1868, and washed out in 1878. It took its name from the fact that it was built in opposition to Mallagh's Wharf, which was located at Cave Landing, today's Pirates Cove. See La Playa.

Pfost Gulch- Probably named for George and William Pfost, residents of the area in 1892. (Cholame)

Phelan Grove- Named for Jeffry Phelan family, who cleared this public picnic area in a grove of trees on their land near Cambria. No longer in use.

Phillips; school district- This district was founded about 1895. It was probably named for Chauncy Hatch Phillips who was a land speculator and promoter. Phillips helped found the towns of Templeton and Creston. (Estrella)

Phoenix Canyon- Named for James Frederick Phoenix who homesteaded in the canyon. (Tar Spring Ridge)

Pico; creek, rock- Named for Jose de Jesus Pico, who owned the land grant of Rancho Piedra Blanca. (Pico Creek)

Picacho Peak- This is a descriptive Spanish term. It means a peaked or pointed eminence. This mountain is best known for the tales of a lost silver mine the Padres supposedly worked on the mountain. (Oceano)

Piedra Blanca, Piedras Blancas; rocks, point, lighthouse, post office- Name refers to the color of the rocks off this point. It is first recorded by Gudde in an 1836 document. It gave its name to the landgrant which covered this area, and the rocks have retained this name on charts since the 1850's. Piedra Blanca, or its plural, refers to white rock, or rocks. The land grant, in the singular form, was given to Jose de Jesus Pico on January 18, 1840. The lighthouse was built in 1874-75. The post office, with the name in the singular form, was in operation from August 25, 1870 until September 5, 1871, and then re-established, with the name in the plural form, from April 5, 1875 to July 6, 1875. (Piedras Blancas)

Pilitas; mountain, creek, canyon, school district- The school district was formed in 1887, and merged into El

The rocks at Piedras Blancas got their name because of their white color, piedras blancas being white rocks in Spanish.

Dorado in 1910. See Las Pilitas. (Lopez Mountain/ Santa Margarita Lake/ Branch Mountain)

Pillar Rock- This rock is named for its resemblance to a pillar, and is located next to Morro Rock.

Pine Mountain; canyon, spring- There are at least 5 mountains, one canyon, one creek, one ridge and one spring named for the ubiquitous pine tree in the county. In California, Gudde wrote of at least 200 such place names. Pines have had great value for their wood, and have long been recognized for their commercial possibilities. (Shandon/ Cholame Hills/ Estrella/ Pozo Summit/ La Panza/ Atascadero/ Pebblestone Shut-in/ San Simeon)

Pines; post office- This post office was only open from May to August in 1893, and was located 17 miles southeast of Santa Margarita. It took its name from the pine trees in the area.

Piney/Pine Ridge; school district- Named for the nearby pine-covered ridge, the school district was formed about 1891, and merged with the Porter district in 1898. (Lopez Mountain)

Pinole Spring- This is named for its location on the Pinole Ranch. (La Panza NE)

Pipeline Lake- One of the dune lakes in the Oceano dunes, this one was named for the oil pipeline which runs through the area. The pipeline was built before 1910. (Oceano)

Pippin Corner- Located just west of Pozo, this corner was named for the old Pippin Ranch, which covered this area. It was the home of W.T. and Mary Clausen Pippin. Mr. Pippin settled here in 1867. (Santa Margarita Lake)

Pirates Cove- See Cave Landing

Pismo, Pizmo; beach, bench, city, creek, lake, landgrant, school district, state beach- Pismo, a Chumash word first applied to this area meaning asphaltum or tar. It was used by the Mexican government for the Rancho El Pismo, granted to Jose Ortega on November 18, 1840. About one half of the original landgrant was later obtained by John Michael Price, who later subdivided the townsite of Pismo, today's Pismo Beach. Originally spelled with an "s", the name pismo has been spelled with a "z" by some developers and hotel owners. The "s" is correct. (Pismo Beach/ Arroyo Grande NE)

Selected Street Names in Pismo Beach

Dolliver- Named for P.C. Dolliver, early owner of the El Pismo Inn.

Harloe- Named for Captain Marcus Harloe.

Mattie- Named for Mattie Smyer, who operated Mattie's Tavern, today's F. McLintock's Restaurant.

Norma- Named for Norma Dye, an employee of the City of Pismo Beach when the developer of this subdivision came in needing street names. Other names from this group include Elaine (DeWitt), Terry (Brisco), Marian (Mello), and Effie (McDermott).

Pomeroy- Named for A. E. Pomeroy, of Pomeroy and Stimson.

Price- Named for John Michael Price.

Stimson- Named for Charles Stimson, who purchased the El Pismo Inn with A.E. Pomerey in 1887.

Wadsworth- Named for Thomas S. Wadsworth, a real estate agent.

Captain Marcus Harloe, after whom Harloe Street in Pismo Beach is named.

Pismo Caves- see Dinosaur Caves

Placer Creek- This creek, in the La Panza area, was named after Epifanio Trujillo found gold here while getting a drink. This find launched the La Panza gold rush in the late 1870's. (La Panza)

Pleasant Valley; valley, school district- The school district was founded before 1895 and took its name from the valley. (Estrella)

Point Buchon- See Buchon. (Morro Bay South OE W)

Point Estero- See Estero. (Cayucos)

Point Piedras Blancas- See Piedras Blancas. (Piedras Blancas)

Point San Luis- Named for the nearby Mission, town, county, etc. (Port San Luis)

Point Sierra Nevada- Named for the Sierra Nevada, a ship which went down near here in 1869. (Piedras Blancas)

Polar Star; school district- This district was formed in 1887, and merged with Washington in 1915. It was named for the Polar Star Mine, a quicksilver mine, in the area. [Thorndyke]

Poly Canyon- Originally named Brizzolara Canyon, for Bartolo Brizzolara who owned the land, today this is named for the California Polytechnic University at San Luis Obispo, or Cal Poly.

Poorman Canyon- Named for H.W. Poorman and his wife, who purchased the seventy-five acres of the Santa

Manuela Rancho which included the canyon in 1875. The canyon was later thought to be aptly named because of the poor soil in the area. [Ditmas] (Arroyo Grande NE)

Port; school district- This school was just inland from the current gate to Diablo Canyon Nuclear Power Plant. The district was named because it served mainly families connected with Port San Luis. The district was founded in 1910 and suspended in 1938.

Port Harford- This name was applied to the post office at the end of John Harford's wharf in 1882 by the Pacific Coast Steamship Company. It was then applied to the entire San Luis Bay, or Bay of San Luis Obispo. The move by the Steamship Company met with opposition on the part of local residents, who held protest meetings, though to no avail. As late as March 30, 1883, the Tribune continued to editorialize against the name change, though it was well established already. The post office was established on December 26, 1882, and renamed Port San Luis on September 9, 1907. (Port San Luis)

Port San Luis- The Port Harford name was finally dropped from the post office at Port San Luis, or San Luis Bay on September 9, 1907. The next day, September 10, the Port San Luis post office was established, again in the warehouse at the end of Harford's Wharf. The post office lasted until December 31, 1932. The name change represented a belated victory for the local residents which had opposed the Port Harford name change in 1882. (Port San Luis)

Porter; school district- Named for the Porter family, descendants of Isaac Sparks, grantee of the Rancho Huasna. The district was formed in 1887, and merged with the

Huasna district in 1910.

Potrero de San Luis Obispo; landgrant- In Spanish, this means the pasture of San Luis Obispo. The Rancho was used by the Mission for grazing herds.

Potrero Creek- This means pasture creek in Spanish. (Tar Spring Ridge/ Lopez Mountain)

Portuguese Flat- Area south of the cemetery off Higuera and Elks Lane south of San Luis Obispo, named for the Oliveras, a Portuguese family who owned the ranch on the site.(Machado Oral Interview) This was also where the climactic crash scene of the movie "Diamond Jim Brady" was filmed.

Poso Ortega- This is a lake in the Temblor Range, not Ortega Spring. (Packwood Creek)

Pozo; town, post office, school district- This town was named for the area's resemblance to a hole or well. Pozo means well or hole. It was named by George Lingo, the first postmaster, after San Jose was rejected by the post office department. The post office here was established on June 18, 1878, and discontinued on September 30, 1942. [Angel] (Pozo Summit/ Santa Margarita Lake)

Prefumo Canyon; creek- Named for Pietro Benedetto Prefumo, an early resident. (San Luis Obispo/ Morro Bay South/ Pismo Beach)

Price Canyon- This canyon in the south county takes its name from John Michael Price, owner of the Rancho El Pismo and this canyon from about 1850 until his death in 1902. (Pismo Beach/ Arroyo Grande NE)

John Michael Price, important early resident of the county and namesake of Price Canyon and Price Road in Pismo Beach.

Punta de La Laguna; landgrant- This land grant is located almost entirely in Santa Barbara County. A small corner juts into the extreme south end of the county, between the Guadalupe and Nipomo landgrants. The name, in Spanish, means Point of the Lake.

Quail Canyon; flat, spring, water creek- Given the number of quail in the county, and their importance to both commercial and private hunters of the last century, it is not surprising that they give their name to at least four sites in the county. (Cuyama/ Atascadero/ Miranda Pine Mountain/ Shedd Canyon/ Wilson Corner)

Ramona Acres- A subdivision just east of the town of Creston, this was a real estate name based on the ongoing popularity of the book Ramona by Helen Hunt Jackson. The area was subdivided in the 1927 by Mr. and Mrs. Isaac Salomon of San Francisco. [Creston] (Creston)

Ramona Hotel; SP siding- This siding was located at the Ramona Hotel, a large and elegant hotel which occupied the block in San Luis Obispo bounded by Marsh, Essex (today's Johnson), Higuera, and the railroad. The depot still stands, and has been moved to the grounds of the Dallidet Adobe in San Luis Obispo.

Ranchial Creek- Named for the Spanish term for pertaining to a rancho.

Ranchita; school district- This district was formed about 1887. In Spanish, this means small rancho.

Ranchita de Santa Fe; landgrant- In Spanish, this means the small rancho of the Holy Faith. It was located south of San Luis Obispo, and was granted to Victor Linares on September 18, 1842. (Pismo Beach)

Rattlesnake Canyon- Named for the abundance of rattle-snakes in the area. (Port San Luis)

Rector Canyon- Located near Cayucos, this canyon is named for William Rector.

Red Rock; canyon, hills, mountain- Red is the second most popular place name color in California, surpassed only by black. (San Simeon/ Caliente Mountain/ Cholame Valley/ Taylor Canyon/ Tent Hills/ Chimineas Ranch/

Camatta Canyon/ Holland Canyon/ Keystone/ Pebblestone Shut-in)

Red Tanks- A well site on the Carrisa Plain, it took its name from two redwood water tanks at the site which were painted red. The tanks had been installed by Miller and Lux, when the company ran sheep on the ranch. (White Oral History)

Redfield Acres/Woods- see Baywood Park

Reeds; PCR station- Perhaps named for E.L. Reed, whose wife filed for a Homestead in 1877, and who was a member of the San Luis Obispo Grange in 1874.

Reservoir Canyon- Named for the first San Luis Obispo City reservoir, located in this canyon. (San Luis Obispo/ Lopez Mountain)

Rickard's Cove- Small cove at the mouth of Leffingwell Creek, this was named for William and Warren Rickard or Ricard.

Righetti Hill- Also known as Mine Hill, this was named for the Righetti Family, on whose ranch this hill was located. See Mine Hill.

Rinconada; creek, valley, school district- In Spanish, this refers to a corner of land shaped by hills, woods, or a roadway. The school district was formed in 1879, and merged with Santa Margarita in 1918. (Lopez Mountain/ Santa Margarita Lake)

Rocky- As a place name adjective, this refers to the large numbers of rocks in the area. In our county, Rocky Butte, Rocky Gorge, and Rocky Canyon are so named.

(Pebblestone Shut-in/ San Simeon/ Atascadero/ Santa Margarita)

Rodrigues Hot Spring- Named for the Rodrigues family who owned the ranch on which it was located. This spring is better known as the Pecho Hot Spring. See Pecho. [Ahrendt]

Rodriguez Friendship Garden- This was a showplace adobe residence in the Upper Arroyo Grande Valley. It was named for Mrs. Rodriguez, who created the gardens.

Root; post office- This post office was named for its first postmaster, Orville Root. It was so named after Miles, for Miles Station on the Pacific Coast Railway where it was located, was rejected by the Post Office authorities as being too close to other post office names. It operated from January 2, 1883 until September 29, 1894.

Rosaville- Name shown for Cambria on the 1870 San Luis Obispo -Cambria road map. See Cambria.

Round Top Mountain- Named for the shape of the mountain. (Arroyo Grande NE)

Routzahn Park- Now located under Lopez Lake, this county park was named for Rev. Louis C. Routzahn, who operated the largest seed farms in the Arroyo Grande Valley at the turn of the century, and was instrumental in saving a grove of oak trees which later became part of the park. [Strother] (Tar Spring Ranch)

Ruda/Ruder Canyon- Named for the Ruda family, related to Rachel See Calloway of See Canyon, and pioneers of the area. (Port San Luis)

S**alinas;** river, valley, school district- The river is named for the salt marshes, or salinas, near the river's mouth, and was applied to the river before 1795. The school district was formed in 1865, and became part of the Eureka district in 1903. (San Miguel/ Paso Robles/ Templeton/ Atascadero/ Santa Margarita/ Lopez Mountain/ Santa Margarita Lake/ Pozo Summit/ Caldwell Mesa/ Los Muchas Hills/ North Chalone Peak)

Salsipuedes Creek; spring- In Spanish, this means "Get out if you can," and was a popular warning on Spanish maps. (Santa Margarita Lake)

Salt Creek- See The Battleground. (Caldwell Mesa/ Tar Spring Ridge)

San Andreas Fault- This is the Spanish name for Saint Andrew, and was applied to the fault by geologist A. C. Lawson. He took the name from the San Andreas reservoir in San Mateo county. It was used by Lawson and his associates as early as 1883, but not officially designated until 1908. (Frazier Mountain/ Slack Canyon/ La Panza NE/ Smith Mountain/ Priest Valley)

San Bernardo; landgrant, creek- This landgrant was named for Bernard of Clairvaux, a French saint who organized the Second Crusade. The creek was named for the landgrant, which was given to Vicente Canet on February 11, 1840. (Morro Bay North/ Morro Bay South)

San Carpoforo/San Carpojo Creek- The route of the Portolá expedition ran along this creek to start the crossing of the Santa Lucias. Father Crespi named the creek Santa

Humiliana. Its current name dates from a rancho of Mission San Antonio de Padua. Camino de S. Carpoforo is first mentioned on a diseño in 1841. Which Saint Carpoforo the creek is named for is not known. [Gudde]

San Geronimo; landgrant- In Spanish, this is Saint Jerome. The land grant was given to Rafael Villavicencia on July 24, 1842. (Cayucos/ Cayucos OE W/ Cambria/ Cypress Mountain)

San Jacinto Canyon- See Lowe's Canyon

San Jose; school district- This district was formed in 1869, and merged with Pozo in 1902. It takes its name from the San Jose valley.

San Juan Creek; valley, school district- Named for Saint John, this was a popular place name in hispanic California. The school district was formed in 1895, and became part of the Park Hill district in 1901. (Camatta Canyon/ Orchard Peak)

San Luis Hill- This is the hill above the Port San Luis lighthouse, and takes its name from the port. AKA San Luis Gonzaga. (Port San Luis)

San Luis Hot Sulphur Springs- see Sycamore Hot Springs.

San Luis Obispo; mission, city, county, mountain, creek, national forest, bay- The mission's original name, San Luis Obispo de Tolosa, refers to Saint Louis, Bishop of Toulouse. He was a minor saint, but was considered a patron of the monastery in Majorca, Spain, where Father

Serra, Father Crespi, and many of the other early missionaries were from. Though the name was first applied to the Santa Barbara area during the Portolá expedition, as our mission was begun earlier the name was moved. The mission was founded on September 1, 1772. The mission's name was used for the town which grew up around the mission, then for the county, one of the first 27 created in 1850. (San Luis Obispo/ Pismo Beach/ Arroyo Grande NE/ Lopez Mountain/ Port San Luis)

Selected Street Names in San Luis Obispo

Al-Hil- Named for Alfred and Hilda Ferrini, developers of the subdivision.
Alphonso- Named for King Alphonso XIII of Spain.
Andrews- Named for John Pinckney Andrews, pioneer rancher and banker.
Beebee- Named for William L. Beebee, part owner of a lumber yard formerly located in the area and local Judge.
Branch- Named for Francis Ziba Branch, grantee of the Santa Manuela Rancho.
Bridge- Named for the world's largest Bailey Bridge company, located on this street.
Brizzolara- Named for Bartolo Brizzolara, pioneer merchant.
Brook- Originally named Eto, for Tamaji Eto who developed the street, this was renamed Brook during World War II in reaction to the attack on Pearl Harbor by the Japanese, and the subsequent hatred of anything Japanese, whether connected with the country or not.
Buchon- Named for Chief Buchon, a Chumash chief with a large goiter, or buchon in Spanish, on his neck.
Calle Joaquin- Named for Joaquin Pereira, who ran a

dairy in the area.

Chorro- Named for being the road to the Chorro valley.

Dalidio- Named for Florino Dalidio.

Daly- Named for Monsignor Patrick Daly, pastor at Mission San Luis Obispo for 22 years.

Dana- Named for William G. Dana, grantee of the Nipomo Rancho.

Ellen- Named for the mother of Miss Anita Hathway who developed the street.

Felton- Named for Felton Ferrini, whose family developed the subdivision.

Fel-Mar- Named for Felton and Marlene Ferrini.

Ferrini- Named for Alfred and Hilda Ferrini who developed their dairy into this subdivision.

Fixlini- Named for the Fixlini family who developed the subdivision.

Francis- Named for Emperor Franz Josef of Austria.

Garcia- Named for Mr. and Mrs. Manuel Garcia, who ran a dairy in the area.

Harris- Named for Robert R. Harris, county surveyor 1869-1874 and 1882-1883.

Hathway- Named for Dr. Amos R. Hathway, pioneer doctor.

Hays- Named for W. W. Hays, first resident doctor in San Luis Obispo.

Higuera- Named for Thomas Higuera, through whose land the road ran.

Humbert- Named for King Umberto of Italy.

Hutton- Named for William Rich Hutton who surveyed the city in 1850, and served as county surveyor 1850-1852.

Johnson- Named for Charles H. Johnson, who served as Customs Inspector for Port San Luis in 1852, and became a noted landowner in San Luis Obispo.

Leff- Named for Gerhard Leff, pioneer German farmer.

Lima- Named for Maria de Gloria Lima family, who ran a dairy in the area.

Lizzie- Named for Lizzie Deleissigues, granddaughter of the owner of the property.

Madonna- Named for Alex Madonna, contractor and builder of the Madonna Inn.

Marlene- Named for Marlene Ferrini, whose family developed the area.

Marsh- Named for the marsh which existed along this road. This was earlier known as Cienega, Spanish for marsh.

Meinecke- Named for Edward and Dorothea Meinecke, on whose land the subdivision including this street is located.

Mill- Named for the grist mill which was located at the foot of the cuesta.

Miossi- Named for the Miossi family, long time residents of Reservoir Canyon.

Monterey- Named for being the road to Monterey during the mission era, this was originally known as Mission Street during the first years of American San Luis Obispo.

Murray- Named for Walter Murray, lawyer and founder of the San Luis Obispo Tribune.

Orcutt- Named for Peter Orcutt.

Palm- Named for a lone palm tree, one of five planted by Father Antonio Martinez, which survived into the early twentieth century.

Parker- Named for William C. Parker, who mapped the town in 1862.

Pereira- Named for Joaquin Pereira and his wife, who ran a dairy in the area.

Phillips- Named for Chauncey Hatch Phillips, banker and land developer in the county.

Reba- Named for Reba Wilson, friend of Dr. and Mrs. Horace Hagen who developed the area.

Sandercock- Named for William Sandercock, founder of the Sandercock Transfer Company.

Santa Rosa- Named for being the road to the Santa Rosa valley.

Smith- Named for the developer, Elmer Smith.

Stenner- Named for William Stenner, harbor master of Port San Luis in the early 1850's.

Story- Named for George Story, county surveyor 1886-1891.

Tank Farm- Named for the oil tank farm which previously existed along this road.

Vachell- Named for Horace Annesly Vachell, English novelist and resident of San Luis Obispo in the 1880's and 1890's.

Venable- Named for McDowell R. Venable, lawyer and Judge.

William Sandercock, after whom Sandercock Street in San Luis Obispo was named.

San Luisito; landgrant, creek- This landgrant's name refers to the name of the mission. There is no little Saint Louis. The land grant was given to Guadalupe Cantua on August 3, 1841. (Morro Bay South/ San Luis Obispo/ Atascadero)

San Marcos; creek, town, post office, school district- The town, post office, and school district take their name from the creek, which was named for Saint Mark. The earliest appearance of the name is in 1795, where it is noted in a document at Mission Santa Barbara as El Arroyo de San Marcos.(Gudde) The school district was formed about 1889, and merged with Paso Robles in 1934. (Paso Robles/ Adelaida)

San Miguel; mission, canyon, town, post office, landgrant, school district-Spanish for Saint Michael the Archangel, this mission was founded as San Miguel Arcangel on July 25, 1797. The mission's name was later applied to the landgrant, post office, town, and school district. The post office was originally established on January 4, 1860 and discontinued on November 9, 1860. It was re-established on August 7, 1861, and again discontinued on January 30, 1862. It was finally re-established on September 2, 1881, only 10 days after another San Miguel post office, this one in San Francisco, was discontinued in our state. The school district was formed before 1882. (San Miguel/ Paso Robles)

San Miguelito; landgrant- Though this is Spanish for little Saint Michael, it actually refers to the same Saint Michael as above. It is on a map made by Narvaez in 1830, though its earliest reference appears to be an approval to build a chapel on the then-Mission Rancho in 1809. The landgrant was given to Miguel Avila, beginning on April 8, 1839. (Pismo Beach/ Port San Luis)

San Simeon; landgrant, town, post office, school district, bay, rock, creek, point- Named for Saint Simeon, this was the site of a ranch of Mission San Miguel. It was in use as early as 1819. The rancho was granted to Jose Ramon Estrada on October 1, 1842. The bay of this name was known as San Simeon Bay at least as early as 1844, when it is mentioned by Duflot de Mofras. A shore whaling station was established here in the 1850's and the town began to develop. The post office was first established April 23, 1864 and discontinued on May 22, 1865. It was re-established October 2, 1867, though this post office was actually in Cambria, and the name was changed to Cambria on January 10, 1870. Again re-established at the old site of San Simeon on December 29, 1873, it was again discontinued on April 5, 1876. The current post office was

George Hearst's wharf and the town of San Simeon on San Simeon Bay about 1900.

established August 9, 1878, and is still in operation. The school district was formed in 1859 ind merged with the Home district in 1918. (Camb.ia/ San Simeon/ Pico Creek/ Pebblestone Shut-in)

Sand Hill; school district- This area of the Los Osos valley was often called the Sand Hills, because of the large number of sand hills in the area. The school district was formed in 1875 and became the Sunnyside District in 1926.

Santa Fe; school district- Named for the Ranchita Santa Fe land grant, which was near the school district. The district was formed before 1871, and merged with Belleview into the Belleview-Santa Fe district in 1946. Santa Fe is Spanish for holy faith.

Santa Lucia; mountains, wilderness- Name given in December 1602 by Vizcaino to the mountain range which traverses our county. The name refers to Saint Lucy of Syracuse. The name is noted in the Portolá expedition diaries, and was apparently well known at that time. The Santa Lucia Wilderness was the first citizen initiated wilderness created in the country. It was created in 1978. [Miossi] (York Mountain/ Cone Peak/ Cypress Mountain/ Cambria/ Lime Mountain/ Pebblestone Shut-in/ Bryson/ Burnett Peak/ Burro Mountain/ Villa Creek)

Santa Manuela; landgrant, school district, school- The landgrant, from which the name of the school district and school come, was named for Manuela Carlon, the wife of the grantee, Francis Ziba Branch, according to Madge Ditmas. Erwin Gudde, in his California Place Names, says it was named for Saint Manuela whose feast day is June 24. There is probably some truth to both explanations, as few land grants were named for living individuals, but if you could utilize a saint's name, and still honor your wife, it was more acceptable. The school district was formed before 1882. (Tar Spring Ridge/ Nipomo/ Oceano/ Arroyo Grande NE)

Santa Margarita; asistencia, landgrant, town, post office, school district, creek, lake- The first mention of this name is by Anza in 1776, and the name probably refers to Saint Margaret of Cortona, as the rancho is referred to as El Rancho Santa Margarita de Cortona in the De la Guerra papers. The rancho was used by the missionaries of Mission San Luis Obispo before 1790, who built an asistencia, or branch chapel in the area before 1830. The rancho was granted to Joaquin Estrada on September 27, 1841. The post office, established as a ranch post office on April 9, 1867 and discontinued on January 15, 1871, was re-established on January 8, 1875. It, and the town, and school district all take their name from the mission rancho. The school district was known as the Tassajara district when it was formed in 1888, and changed its name to Santa Margarita in 1897. Murphy Street in the town is named for Patrick Murphy who owned the rancho when the town was developed. (Santa Margarita)

Santa Maria Valley; river- This area straddles the Santa Maria River, the southern boundary of San Luis Obispo County. It was a popular Spanish placename, referring to Mary, the mother of Christ. (Pt. Sal/ Guadalupe/ Oceano/ Nipomo/ Santa Maria/ Twitchell Dam/ Sisquoc/ Foxen Canyon/ Twitchell Dam)

Santa Rita Creek- This was probably named for the Santa Rita Ranch, located on the creek. Santa Rita refers to Saint Rita of Cassis. (York Mountain)

Santa Rosa; landgrant, creek, valley, school district, reef- This was named for either Saint Rosa de Lima, a Dominican saint, or Saint Rosa de Viterbo, a Franciscan saint of the 13th century. [Gudde] The school district was formed in 1866. (Cambria/ Cypress Mountain/ Port San Luis)

Santa Ysabel; landgrant, hot springs- Named for the Arroyo de Santa Ysabel, or stream of Saint Elizabeth, Queen of Portugal. The stream was known by this name at least as early as 1797. (Templeton/ Creston/ Paso Robles/ Estrella)

Sapaque Valley- Kroeber lists this as the name of a valley on the Monterey/San Luis Obispo county line. He considered the term Salinan, though without any known meaning. [Kroeber]

Saucelito Canyon- In Spanish, this refers to a little grove of willow trees, which were often found around water sources. The canyon was named for Henry Ditmas's Saucelito canyon. [Ditmas] (Tar Spring Ridge)

Saucito Spring- In Spanish, this means little willow spring. Willows often grew around waterholes. (Chimineas Ranch)

Schau Peak- This is probably named for the pioneer Mehlschau family. (Nipomo)

Schoolhouse Canyon- Located between Pismo Beach and Arroyo Grande, this is named for the Oak Park School which was at the mouth of the canyon. A second canyon by this name is located in the southeast of the county. (Caliente Mountain/ Peak Mountain/ Bates Canyon)

Scott Rock- Located on Santa Rosa Creek Road, this rock is named for Greenup Scott, an early settler. (Cambria)

Sea Gull Rock- see Bird Rock

Section Base- A military designation, this refers to the Naval base established at Morro Bay in 1942. A section base was used for coastal defense, and was assigned small boats which were to patrol the coast line. A post office of this name was established November 1, 1942 and discontinued July 8, 1943.

See Canyon- Named by Rachel See Calloway, an early resident of the canyon, for her family name. She is said to have traded a mule for the canyon. (Pismo Beach/ Port San Luis/ Morro Bay South)

Sellars Portrero- Located in the La Panza area, this means Sellars pasture. (Pozo Summit)

Serrano; SP siding- Named for the pioneer Serrano family, this was a water station near Stenner Creek and was listed as early as 1894 in the SP station listing. Miguel Serrano was a son-in-law of Estevan Quintana who had acquired the property during the 1820's. (San Luis Obispo)

Shamel County Park- Located in Cambria, this park is

named for Ray Shamel who was a Cambria businessman and promoter. He came to Cambria in 1928. The park was originally known as Cambria County Park. [Cambrian 2-27-1986]

Shandon; town, post office, valley, flat, school district-This town was originally named Sunset, by its founder Charles Tobey. According to an article in the San Luis Obispo Tribune of August 5, 1891, the name was chosen from the poem Shandon Bells. According to A.L. Morrison, Dr. John Hughes is credited with suggesting the name. The Starkey post office moved to the new town in 1891. The school district was formed about 1898 when the Starkey school was moved to the town. See Starkey. (Shandon/ Cholame)

Selected Streets in Shandon

Camatti- Named for the Camatti Ranch.
Cholame- Named for the landgrant.
Truesdale- Named for the pioneer Truesdale family of Shandon.

Shannon Hill- A small hill just south of downtown Arroyo Grande, this is named for Annie Gray Shannon, who had the Hillcrest Farm here.

Shark Inlet- Located at the south end of Morro Bay, this area's name engenders some confusion. Some have thought this was the site of a break in the sand spit, but geological and archaeological evidence show that this was not the case within historic times.

Sheep Camp; canyon, creek- The raising of sheep was an important part of the county's ranching economy from Mexican times on, and is reflected in the number of sites named for sheep or sheep camps. These are often located in isolated areas because of the amount of land needed for a large sheep raising operation. (Painted Rock/ Estrella/ Shandon/ York/ Los Machos Hills)

Sheerin's Station- Thomas J. Sheerin purchased Cashin's Station, and it was renamed for him. See Cashin's Station. [Daily Republic, November 26, 1888]

Sheid/Shedd Canyon- Named for W. T. Sheid who homesteaded the area before 1869. He chose the area for a natural spring, which was already the site of a small Native American village. Some accounts list his name as Shedd. (Shedd Canyon/ Shandon)

Shell Beach; beach, subdivision, post office- The beach known as Shell Beach was originally known as Rocky Beach at the turn of the century. When the subdivision was laid out in 1926 by Floyd Calvert, it was called Shell Beach, as was the post office which existed as an independent post office, from June 14, 1939 to October 6, 1967, when it became a branch of Pismo Beach. The area is today within the City of Pismo Beach. (Pismo Beach)

Shell Creek- Named for the large number of fossil oyster shells found along the creek's length. (Camatta Ranch)

Sherwood Field- Airport east of Paso Robles, used by the Army Air Corps during World War II. It was named for George Sherwood who was born in 1897 and died in 1935.

He was an airmail pilot whose plane crashed just after takeoff from today's Burbank airport. He had been with the 115th Observation Corps, part of the 40th Division, which was later stationed at the field. It is no longer in operation, and the land is part of a subdivision. [Quinn]

Shimmon/Simmon Canyon- This canyon was named for Francis M. Shimmon, who operated the Shimmon ranch in the canyon. (Cholame Hills/ Shandon)

Silver Lake- Located near Creston, this is probably named for the apparent color of the lake. (Santa Margarita)

Simmler; townsite, post office, school district- Named for John Jacob Simmler, postmaster and businessman in San Luis Obispo. The story runs that Simmler offered to help A. F. Hubbard get a new post office on the Carrisa Plain, if it would be named for him. Hubbard agreed, and the post office of Simmler was established on July 21, 1887. It was discontinued on September 30, 1930. The school district was formed about 1891, and changed its name to Carrisa Plains in 1954. (Simmler)

Small Twin Lake- See Big Twin. (Oceano)

Smith Creek- This may take its name from O.K. Smith, who was presumed drowned here in 1871. No body was ever found. (Cayucos)

Smith Island- Named for Joe and Mattie Smith, who lived on the island from 1884 until 1894. [Olsen] (Port San Luis)

Soda Lake- Originally called Salt Lake, for the salty taste of the water, this normally dry lake on the Carrisa Plain had its name changed after the deposits on the surface of the lake bed were analyzed. They were found to be high in soda, and were mined in the early part of the twentieth century. (Chimineas Ranch/ Painted Rock/ Simmler)

Someo; school district- This district was formed before 1882. It takes its name from the town of Someo in Canton Ticino in Switzerland. Many of the earliest Italian-Swiss emigrants to San Luis Obispo County were from this, and other nearby towns.

Spooner's Cove- This cove is now part of the Montaña De Oro State Park. It takes its name from the Spooner family, which began ranching this land in 1892, eventually holding 9,000 acres. Before the arrival of the Spooner family, the cove was called Buchon Landing. See Buchon. See photo - next page.

Spring; School District- This district was formed before 1882 and merged with Shandon in 1899. It was named for Sheid Spring near Shandon. See Sheid Spring.

Springs- This post office was established at the Sycamore or San Luis Hot Springs on May 18, 1900. It was not until two months later that mail began being delivered there by the Pacific Coast Railway which ran past the site and the post office was discontinued on November 15, 1900. Its name is not derived from a natural hot springs, but rather from a failed oil well which brought in hot water. See Sycamore Hot Springs.

Squire Canyon- Named for the Gevin Squire family,

Reverend A. B. Spooner, whose name is preserved in Spooner's Cove on the Montaña de Oro State Park.

early residents of the canyon. Their family home was located where Highway 101 is today, and was moved to the Avila [Ontario] Hot Springs when the highway was enlarged. Gevin Squire was an English immigrant who was naturalized in 1891. (Pismo Beach)

Starkey; post office, school- This post office was named by Nicholas Mayer, the first postmaster, for a friend of his. Starkey, according to Linda Young's paper on the history of the community, was a claim jumper, and the name did not meet with the approval of local citizens. It was established on December 14, 1885, and moved to the new Shandon settlement and renamed on June 30, 1891. See Shandon.

Steele's; PCR stop- This was named for the Steele family. George and Edgar Steele came to San Luis Obispo County in 1866 and started the dairy industry. This stop on the Pacific Coast Railway was in the Edna Valley, on part of the Corral de Piedra landgrant which had been purchased by the Steeles.

Steele Canyon- In the Huasna area, this canyon was named for early resident Thomas Steele and his wife. [Ditmas]

Steiner Creek- Probably named for George "Jack" Steiner, born in the area in 1879, or his father Charles Alfred Steiner. (Cambria/ Cypress Mountain)

Stenner Creek- Sometimes misspelled Steiner Creek, though not the one listed above, it was named for William Stenner who lived in the area. Stenner was from England,

and arrived in the county in 1850, becoming Harbormaster at Port San Luis in the 1850's. This creek was called the Arroyo de la Huerta Viejo, or creek of the old orchard, referring to the mission orchard which it ran through, on the 1874 County Map. (San Luis Obispo)

Stevens Canyon- This canyon in the Huasna area, also known as Rocky Canyon, is named for Mort Stevens who had a ranch in the canyon. [Porter] (Huasna Peak)

Stowe; school district- Probably named for Ida Hollister Stowe, daughter of John Hollister, on whose ranch the district was partially located. The district was formed about 1878.

Strother Park- This park just east of Arroyo Grande is named for Newell Strother, longtime editor and publisher of the Arroyo Grande Herald Recorder newspaper.

Suey; landgrant, post office, creek- This name is taken from the Chumash word Swey, meaning tarweed. The Rancho Suey was granted on April 6, 1837, to Ramona Carrillo Pacheco de Wilson, and straddles the San Luis Obispo and Santa Barbara County lines today. It was one of the first three ranchos granted in our county. A post office was established on October 12, 1870 in Santa Barbara County, but because of a boundary line adjustment became part of our county on March 13, 1872. The post office was discontinued on April 19, 1875. (Twitchell Dam/ Tepusquet Canyon/ Santa Maria/ Nipomo/ Huasna Peak)

Sulphur; canyon, spring- There are at least four sulphur springs, two sulphur canyons, a black sulphur spring and many other sites named for a sulphurous smell in our county. (Bradley/ Tierra Redonda Mountain/ New Cuyama/ Wells Ranch/ Branch Mountain/ Caliente Mountain/ Templeton)

Summit; school district, canyon, creek , PCR stop- The school district was located in the north county and was formed in 1872. The district was located along the summit of the coast range east of San Miguel. In the south county, the Pacific Coast Railway had a station by this name at the summit of the climb to the top of the Nipomo Mesa. (York Mountain/Arroyo Grande)

Sunderland; school district- This district was formed before 1882, and merged with the Lincoln district to form the Adelaida district in 1948. Milton Sunderland, a son of Thomas Sunderland, owner and namesake of the Sunderland Quicksilver Mine, was a well known resident of the area, and the first school house was built on his property. The mine later became the Klau Mine, after its purchase by Karl Klau. See Klau.

Sunnyside; school district- This district was formed about 1891. (Morro Bay South)

Sunset- See Shandon/ Starkey.

Sunset Palisades- A modern real estate promotional name. See Oilport. (Pismo Beach)

Sunshine Beach- This failed townsite was developed by Norman Harrison and D. R. Oliver in 1893. The map of the town was filed with the county on April 5, 1893. The town was to be south of the town of El Moro on Morro Bay. The name is a real estate promotional name. See El Moro.

Swallow Rock- Large rock near the Green Valley Road junction on Highway 1 near Cambria. Named for the large number of swallows which nested on the rock.

Sweet Springs- A fresh water spring in the sand hills at the west end of the Los Osos valley. Named for its fresh water.

Sycamore Canyon; creek, spring, ridge- These are all named for the western sycamore. Sycamores prefer dry creeks, which accounts for the proliferation of sycamore canyons. There are at least five canyons with this name in the county. (Morro Bay North/ Nipomo/ Lopez Mountain/ San Luis Obispo/ Morro Bay South/ Miranda Pine Mountain/ Taylor Canyon/ Chimineas Ranch/ Branch Mountain)

Sycamore Hot Springs- This hot springs resort in the Avila valley, inland from Avila Beach, was the site of a failed Oil Well drilled in May 1886, which brought in hot water rather than oil. Originally known as Oil Wells, because of the original failure, it was renamed the Sycamore Springs for the huge sycamore trees in the area. It has also been known as the San Luis Hot Sulphur Springs and the Sycamore Hot Sulphur Springs. (Pismo Beach)

Syncline Hill- This hill was given this name by the Geographic Board in 1909. A syncline is a geologic fold in a strata. (California Valley)

Tajea Spring; flat- This may be from the Spanish taja, meaning a cut or incision. This would be in keeping with a spring. (Branch Mountain)

Tank Farm- There are actually two Tank Farms in the county, though the best known is just south of San Luis Obispo on Tank Farm Road. The area takes its name from the large number of oil storage tanks in the area. This was the site of the infamous Tank Farm Fire of 1926, when a 1,000,000 barrel tank was ignited in a lightning storm, exploding with enough force to cause damage throughout San Luis Obispo. The fire killed three, and to put out the burning oil, it was finally allowed to run down San Luis Obispo Creek to San Luis Bay. This was actually the second Tank Farm Fire in the county, however, as a 35,000 barrel tank on the hill above Avila, had been ignited by a lightning storm in 1908. Both fires were caused by the tanks not having lightning arresters on the tanks, in both

A circa 1900 advertisement for the Sycamore Hot Springs. The site has had many names, and was originally known as the Oil Wells because the original hot spring was a failed oil well.

cases because designers did not consider that lightning occured in our county.

Tar Spring; creek, canyon, ranch, ridge- This site and ranch takes its name from the natural asphaltum, or tar, springs in the area. The tar was used by the Chumash to caulk baskets and canoes, as well as a natural glue for adding decoration to stone, wood, bone, and shell items. (Tar Spring Ridge/ Arroyo Grande NE)

Tarantula Hill- In Atascadero, this hill was noted during the 1904 war games on the Atascadero Ranch. It takes its name from the large number of tarantulas in the area.

Tasajaro/Tassajara Canyon; school district- In Span-

The original Tar Spring on the Tar Spring Ranch, as shown in the May 5, 1894, San Luis Tribune Railroad Special Edition.

The main street of Templeton, named for Templeton Crocker, about 1915.

---

ish, this refers to a place where meat is cut into strips and dried, or jerked. See Santa Margarita. (Atascadero)

Temblor Range- Temblor in Spanish means earthquake. This range is named for the San Andreas fault. [Still]

Temettate/Temettati Creek; ridge- This creek is first shown on the diseño of the Rancho Bolsa de Chamisal. The word is derived from the term temetate, a Mexican curved stone used as a mortar. [Gudde] (Nipomo/ Huasna Peak)

Templeton; town, post office, school district- This town was subdivided and promoted by the West Coast Land Company, which was partially owned by the Southern Pacific Railroad. It was originally to be named Crocker, for Templeton Crocker. When the name was found to have great negative connotations within the rural community, which was not pleased with the Southern Pacific Railroad, the name was changed to Templeton. (Templeton)

Selected Streets in Templeton

Blackburn- Named for the Blackburn Brothers who owned the Paso de Robles rancho.
Crocker- Named for Templeton Crocker.
James- Named for Drury James, who owned the Paso de Robles rancho with the Blackburn Brothers.
Wilhoit- Named for Reverend Wilhoit

Terrace Hill- Located next to the Southern Pacific yards in San Luis Obispo, this was originally promoted as a subdivision for railroad employees, first being called The Terraced Hill. According to local historian Dan Krieger, this hill was named for terraces built to control erosion. The hill's name was later shortened to Terrace Hill. (San Luis Obispo)

Thompson Spring- There are two Thompson Springs in the county. One located in the Lopez area is probably named for R. A. Thompson, who operated a boy's home in the area. [Strother] A second is located in the Simmler area of the Carrisa Plain. (Branch Mountain/ Simmler)

Thyle; SP siding- This station appears in the 1904 SP station list, but not in the 1899. It is shown as one mile south of the Cuesta summit station in the 1918 SP station list, and is between tunnels 6 and 7. This was the site of a railroad worker camp during the building of the tunnels on the Cuesta. It was probably named for the Thyle family, whose son, Irvine, worked for the Southern Pacific. He lost an arm in an accident in Paso Robles.(San Luis Obispo)

Tiber; SP station, canyon- This station is shown on the 1918 SP station list, and is named for the Tiber Oil

Company who discovered oil in Price Canyon about 1901. The oil field still bears the Tiber name. It was located eight miles south of San Luis Obispo, near the Ormonde road undercrossing. [Miossi] (Arroyo Grande NE)

Tierra Redonda Mountain- In Spanish, this means round land, and refers to the peak. It was also applied to the rancho, which was granted to Christian Indians from Mission San Miguel, but the grant was not upheld under American law. (Tierra Redonda)

Toro Creek- Toro is the Spanish word for bull. Two Toro Canyons exist in the county, one near Morro Bay and one near Pozo. (Morro Bay North/ Santa Margarita Lake/ Pozo Summit)

Trout Creek- There are two creeks in the county with this name. Trout is tied with salmon as the most popular fish placename in California. [Gudde] (Lopez Mountain/ Caldwell Mesa/ Santa Margarita/ Pozo Summit/ Santa Margarita Lake)

Turtle Rock- This rock is named for its resemblance to a turtle.

Twin Lakes; big, small- See Big Twin. (Oceano)

Twisselman Lake- Named for the pioneer Twisselman family who are still prominent in the area. (Orchard Peak)

Twitchell Dam; reservoir- Named for Santa Maria attorney and Santa Barbara Supervisor T. A. "Cap" Twitchell, a long-time supporter of the dam project. [Carlson] (Twitchell Dam/ Huasna Peak/ Nipomo)

U nion; town, post office, school district- This school district was formed about 1893, and later merged with Paso Robles. The name came from the location of the settlement at the union of the Paso Robles, Shandon and Creston roads. [Home Demonstration Day 1958] (Estrella)

Upton Canyon- Named for Roscoe E. Upton, who had a ranch in the area. [White] (Camatta Canyon/ Camatta Ranch/ Shedd Canyon)

Valley Township- Originally created as the Estrella Township, the name was changed in 1888 to clear up any confusion with the Estrella post office in the township. Named for the Salinas Valley. [Tribune, 7-4-1888]

Van Gordon Creek- Named for the Ira Van Gorden family. (Cambria/ Pebblestone Shut-in)

Van Ness Canyon- Probably named for James Van Ness, who died in 1872 while serving as State Senator from our county, this canyon is located in the Cuesta Ridge off Highway 41.

Vaquero Spring- Located near Pozo, this spring is named for the vaqueros, or cowboys, who used it while working for the ranches in the area.

Vaquero Flat; reservoir- The Vaquero flats are near the Huasna valley, and are probably named because the local vaqueros used the area. The reservoir is now known as Twitchell Reservoir, though it is shown as Vaquero Reservoir on the 1957 Division of Forestry San Luis Obispo County map. (Huasna Peak)

Vasa- This town was laid out south of the present city of Atascadero by the Eureka Improvement Company for Swedish immigrants. It was named for Vasa, Sweden. See Eureka.

Vasquez Creek- Near Lopez Lake, this is named for Antonio Vasquez who homesteaded the property on the creek. It is also known as Basquez or Vasques creek. (Tar

Spring Ridge/ Lopez Mountain/ Arroyo Grande NE)

Verde; canyon, school district, PCR stop- In Spanish, this means green. This school district was formed about 1895, and merged with Arroyo Grande in 1953. (Arroyo Grande NE)

Villa Creek- The creek near Cayucos was originally known as Rafael Villa Creek, and later shortened to it current name. Rafael Villavicencia was the grantee of the San Geronimo Rancho. A second Villa Creek is located in the Lopez area. (Cayucos/ Cypress Mountain/ Arroyo Grande NE/ Lopez Mountain)

Vineyard Canyon; springs, creek- There are at least two Vineyard Canyons in San Luis Obispo County. The one near San Miguel was named for the Mission San Miguel vineyard, which is still shown on this creek on the 1874 County Map. According to an oral interview with early day resident Ella Adams, "The name goes back to mission days when in 1815 a 3-room adobe with tile roof was built for the vineyardists to care for the mission vineyards, orchards, and garden at Vineyard Springs." A second Vineyard Canyon in the Port San Luis area is also known as Irish Canyon. (San Miguel/ Ranchito Canyon/ Stockdale Mountain/ Port San Luis)

Vista del Mar- Subdivision promoted in Santa Maria between 1905 and 1911. The townsite was located just south of Oso Flaco Lake, and was never successful. In Spanish, the name means view of the sea, and was a real estate promotional name.

Warden Lake- Named for H. M. Warden, pioneer area farmer and rancher. (Morro Bay South)

Washington; school district- Originally this school district covered all of the area between the coastal range and the ocean from the Monterey County line to the Arroyo de Padre Juan. In 1905 it was reduced to an area located two miles north of the Piedras Blancos lighthouse on Arroyo de los Chinos. This district was formed in 1870, and was probably named for George Washington.

Wells Siding; SP station- See Wellsona.

Wellsona; SP stop- This is shown as Wells Siding in the 1887 Southern Pacific station list, but the name has changed to Wellsona in the 1894 SP station listing. (Paso Robles)

West Los Berros; school district- This district, founded in 1895 and merged with Los Berros in 1899, was located west of the Los Berros district.

West Pecho; school district- This district was formed in 1906, and merged with Sunnyside in 1912. It takes its name from its location.

West Tuley Springs- This is named for the Tuley family, who were prominent ranchers and populists in the area at the turn of the century. Jacob Tuley later published and edited the Reasoner, a populist newspaper in San Luis Obispo. (Shandon)

Whale Rock; dam- According to local tradition, this was

the site used by shore whalers for spotting whales off the Cayucos coast. The application of the name to the dam was a matter of some controversy, as many area residents felt that it should have been called Old Creek Dam. [Miossi] (Cayucos)

Whaler's, Whaler Island- This island, now part of the breakwater at Port San Luis, is named for the early shore whalers who lived on the rock. The main whaling station was actually at the point below the Port San Luis Obispo lighthouse. (Port San Luis)

White; creek, lake (dune lake), rock, well- White is the third most popular color place name in California, after black and red. Rocks of this name are located off today's Sunset Palisades and off Cambria. See also Piedras Blancas. [Gudde] (Oceano/ Cholame/ Pismo Beach/ Cambria)

White Canyon; spring- This was probably named for Ellen E. White, daughter of Mauricio Gonzales. Gonzales was granted the Rancho Cholame on February 7, 1844, and it was patented to his daughter on April 1, 1865. She sold the ranch to W. W. Hollister in 1867. (Cholame Valley/ Cholame)

White Point- The site of today's Morro Bay Museum of Natural History, this point is named for Frederick White, an early supervisor of the county. [Bailey and Gates] (Morro Bay South)

Whiterock Bluff- See white. (Caliente Mountain)

Whitley Gardens- Named for Mr. Whitley, the southern California developer who promoted the development. The area had earlier been the site of the 15 Mile House, a roadhouse. Whitley was responsible for bringing the first electricity to the area. Whitley was also said to have been involved with Horace Wilcox who developed Hollywood. See 15 Mile House. [PR Cent./Davies] (Estrella/ Shandon)

Wild Cherry Canyon- The wild cherry, under the Indian name Islay, also appears on a small hill east of San Luis Obispo. (Pismo Beach/ Port San Luis)

Wild Hog Canyon; creek- Perhaps named for Jim Allen's hog ranch. He used domestic hogs to capture wild hogs and fatten them between 1905 and 1907, and drove the herd from the canyon to Arroyo Grande for sale. [Strother] (Branch Mountain)

Wild Horse Canyon; spring- Probably named for the number of wild horses, a boon to ranchers, in the area. (Camatta/ Camatta Ranch/ Cholame Hills)

Willow; creek, lake, spring, canyon- The willow usually grows near running water. This makes it a popular placename throughout the state of California, as running water was often critical to agricultural success. There are at least two creeks, four springs, one lake and one canyon with this name Other willow related names in the county include Willow Springs Canyon, Five Willow Spring and the Spanish versions of Saucito and Saucelito. [Gudde] (La Panza/ Cayucos/ Morro Bay North/ York Mountain/ Oceano/ Cuyama/ Camatta Ranch/ Atascadero/ La Panza Ranch/ Cholame Hills)

Wittenberg Canyon- Named for Newton and William Wittenberg. [Ditmas] (Tar Spring Ridge/ Santa Margarita Lake)

Wittenberg Creek- Named for David F. Wittenberg, an early settler in the area. He purchased land from the Steele Brothers. His holdings are shown on the 1874 County Map. (Tar Spring Ridge/ Santa Margarita Lake)

Wood Canyon- There are at least two canyons by this name in the county. Given the importance of wood in American life, this is a favorite American place name. [Gudde] (Tent Hills/ Shandon/ Shedd Canyon)

Wyss Creek- Named for Otto Wyss and his family, who farmed in the area. Wyss also served as postmaster for Adelaida. The creek is in the Adelaida region.

Yeguas Creek- Yeguas means mare, or female horse in Spanish. It takes its name from Las Yeguas Spring, named during the mission era because of a band of wild mares which were followed to find the spring. [MacLean] (La Panza NE/ Las Yeguas Ranch)

Yerba Buena Creek- In Spanish, this means good herb, and refers to the *Micromeria Chamissonis* plant. (Lopez Mountain/ Santa Margarita)

Ynocenta- This failed 1887 boom era townsite was just inland of Avila. It was named for Miguel Avila's wife, Ynocenta. Though lots were sold initially, no town ever developed on the site.

York Mountain- Named for the York family, founders of the York Mountain Winery, and relatives of the Cass family of Cayucos. (York Mountain)

Zemorra Creek- This name may be a corruption of zarzamora, Spanish for blackberry bush. (Carneros Rocks/ Las Yeguas Ranch)

BIBLIOGRAPHY

BOOKS:

Adams, Carole, Guide to Historic Cambria, 1986, Vulture Vista Publications, Cambria

Angel, Myron, History of San Luis Obispo County, California, with Illustrations and Biographical Sketches of its Prominent Men and Pioneers., Fourth Edition, 1986, EZ Nature Books, San Luis Obispo

Applegate, Dr. Richard, *An Index of Chumash Placenames*, in *Papers on the Chumash*, Occasional Paper #9, 1975, San Luis Obispo County Historical Society, pgs. 19-46

Bailey, Richard C., Kern County Place Names, 1967, Kern County Historical Society, Bakersfield

Ballard, Helen M., *San Luis Obispo County in Spanish and Mexican Times*, in *California History Quarterly*, Volume 1, Pages 152-172, 1922, California Historical Society, San Francisco

Bettencourt, Joseph, et al., The Pozo Diary, 1983, South County Historical Society, Arroyo Grande

Blakley, E.R. and Barnette, Karen, Historical Overview of Los Padres National Forest, 1985, Los Padres National Forest, n.p.

Cameron, William R., *Rancho Santa Margarita of San Luis Obispo*, in *California Historical Society Quarterly*, Volume XXXVI, Number 1, Pages 1-20, 1957, California Historical Society, San Francisco

Carlson, Vada F., This Is Our Valley, 1959, Westernlore Press, Los Angeles, sponsored by the Santa Maria Valley Historical Society

Carpenter, E. J. and Storie, R. Earl, Soil Survey of The Paso Robles Area, California, 1928, United States Department of Agriculture, Washington

Cavanagh, Lulu, Timothy Cavanagh and Descendants, (1974), Lulu Cavanagh, np

Clark, Donald Thomas, Monterey County Place Names: A Geographical Dictionary, 1991, Kestrel Press, Carmel Valley, CA

Coffman, Taylor, Hearst's Dream, 1989, EZ Nature Books, San Luis Obispo

Cowan, Robert G., Ranchos of California: A List of Spanish Concessions 1775-1822 and Mexican Grants 1822-1846, 1977, The Historical Society of Southern California, Los Angeles

Creston Women's Club, Creston, 1884-1984, 1984, Creston Women's Club, Creston

Curry, Elliot, La Vista, Volume 3, Numbers 3 and 4, June 1973 and January 1974, San Luis Obispo County Historical Society, San Luis Obispo

Dana, Alonzo P., The Dana, Carrillo, Boronda, Deleissigues and Munoz Families in California, 1966, Alonzo Dana, np

Darling, Curtis, Kern County Place Names, 1988, Kern County Historical Society, Fresno, CA

Dart, Louisiana Clayton, What's in a Name?, 1979, Mission Federal Savings, San Luis Obispo

de Rivas, F.M., edit., Diccionario Salva'-Webster / Salva'-Webster English-Spanish and Spanish-English Dictionary, 1899, Laird and Lee, Chicago

Diller, J. S. and others, Guidebook of the Western United States: Part D. The Shasta Route and Coast Line, 1916, Government Printing House, Washington

Dillon, Richard H., La Panza, 1960, William P. Wreden, San Francisco

Ditmas, Madge C., According to Madge, 1983, South County Historical Society, Arroyo Grande

El Paso de Robles Area Historical Society and the Daily Press, Centennial Family Memories, 1989, Daily Press, Paso Robles

Englehardt, Zepherin, San Miguel Arcangel, the Mission on the Highway, 1931, Mission Santa Barbara, Santa Barbara

Englehardt, Zepherin, Mission San Luis Obispo in the Valley of the Bears, 1963, W. T. Genns, Santa Barbara

Farris, Glenn, *Finding Cholame, Tisagues, Camate, Lhuegue and Sataoyo, Five Villages on the Salinan-Chumash Border*, unpublished ms., (1993), used by the courtesy of the author

Fisher, Anne B., The Salinas; Upside Down River, 1945, Farrar and Rinehart, New York

Gudde, Erwin G., California Place Names; The Origin and Etymology of Current Geographic Place Names, Third Edition, 1969, University of California Press, Berkeley, Los Angeles, London

Hall-Patton, Mark P., Various Columns from the *San Luis Obispo Telegram-Tribune* newspaper, 1986-1993

Hamilton, Geneva, Where the Highway Ends, 1974, Padre Productions, San Luis Obispo

Hanna, Phil Townsend, The Dictionary of California Land Names, Second Edition, 1951, Automobile Club of Southern California, Los Angeles

Heiser, R. F., edit., California Indian Linguistic Records; The Mission Indian Vocabularies of Alphonse Pinart, Anthropological Records 15:1, 1952, University of California Press, Berkeley

Klar, Kathryn A, *An Addendum to Applegates's "Chumash Place Names", Occasional Paper #9,* in *Los Osos Junior High School Site 4-SLO-214, Occasional Paper 11*, 1977, San Luis Obispo County Archaeological Society, pgs. 52-54

Krieger, Daniel E., Various Columns from the *San Luis Obispo Telegram-Tribune* newspaper, 1981-1993

Krieger, Daniel E., Looking Backward into the Middle Kingdom, San Luis Obispo County, Second Edition, 1990, EZ Nature Books, San Luis Obispo

Kroeber, A. L., California Place Names of Indian Origin, 1916, University of California Publications in American Archaeology and Ethnography, Vol. 12, Number 2, Pages 31-69, University of California Press, Berkeley

Larson, Coleen Handforth, A History of the Hollister Adobe, 1971, Cuesta College, San Luis Obispo

Lee, Georgia, et al., An Uncommon Guide to San Luis Obispo County California, 1977, Padre Productions, San Luis Obispo

Los Angeles Directory Company, <u>San Luis Obispo City and County Directory</u>, 1913, 1914, Los Angeles Directory Company, Los Angeles

Lynch, James, <u>With Stevenson to California</u>, 1954, Biobooks, Oakland

MacGillivray, Fraser, <u>Adelaida</u>, unpublished manuscript used by permission of the author

MacLean, Angus, <u>The Ghosts of Frank and Jesse James, and Other Stories</u>, 1987, Bear Flag Books, San Luis Obispo

Marinacci, Barbara and Rudy, <u>California's Spanish Place-Names; What They Mean and How They Got Here</u>, 1980, Presidio Press, San Rafael

Mason, J. Alden, <u>The Ethnology of the Salinan Indians</u>, University of California Publications in American Archaeology and Ethnology, Vol. 10, No. 4, December 14, 1912, University of California Press, Berkeley

Mason, J. Alden, <u>The Language of the Salinan Indians</u>, University of California Publications in American Archaeology and Ethnology, Vol. 14, No. 1, January 10, 1918, University of California Press, Berkeley

McIntosh, George R., <u>Mc's Stage Line</u>, 1972, George McIntosh, np

McMillan, Don, and Young, Linda A., *Homesteaders in the Shandon Valley*, in *La Vista*, Volume 3, Number 1, June 1972, San Luis Obispo County Historical Society, San Luis Obispo

McNary, Laura Kelly, <u>California Spanish and Indian Place Names</u>, 1931, Wetzel Publishing Company, Los Angeles

Miossi, Harold, Somnolent Cape, *The Story of the Pecho Coast*, from *La Vista*, Volume 3, Number 2, January 1973, San Luis Obispo County Historical Society, San Luis Obispo

Miossi, Harold, Interview 11-19-93, unrecorded, with Author, regarding review of manuscript

Moreno, H.M., <u>Moreno's Dictionary of Spanish-Named California Cities and Towns</u>, 1916, Holmes Book Co., Los Angeles

Morrison, Annie L., <u>History of San Luis Obispo County and Envi-</u>

rons, California, with Biographical Sketches of the Leading Men and Women of the County and Environs Who have been Identified with the Growth and Development of the Section from the Early Days to the Present, 1917, Historic Record Company, Los Angeles

Nicholson, Loren, Rails Across the Ranchos, 1980, Valley Publishers, Fresno

Olsen, Doris, *South County - the way it was*, reprints of newspaper columns from the *San Luis Obispo Telegram-Tribune*, nd, (Hubbard Printing), (Arroyo Grande)

Priestley, Herbert Ingram, trans., *A Historical, Political, and Natural Description of California by Pedro Fages; Written for the Viceroy in 1775*, 1937, University of California, Berkeley

Radcliffe, Louise, Homestead Declarations in San Luis Obispo County, Ca., 1860-1884, 1979, Central Coast Genealogical Society, San Luis Obispo

Rawson, Lura, Various Columns from the *San Luis Obispo Telegram- Tribune* newspaper, 1987-1990

Robinson, W. W., The Story of San Luis Obispo County, 1957, Title Insurance and Trust Company, Los Angeles

Salley, H. E., History of California Post Offices, 1849-1976, 1977, H. E. Salley, La Mesa

San Luis Obispo County, Great Register of Registered Voters, 1867, 1871, 1890, 1892, various printers, various places

Sanchez, Nellie Van Der Grift, Spanish and Indian Place Names of California, 1914, A. M. Robertson, San Francisco

Santa Lucia Chapter, Sierra Club, San Luis Obispo County Trail Guide, Second Edition, 1989, Santa Lucia Chapter of the Sierra Club, San Luis Obispo

Sealock and Seely, Bibliography of Place-Name Literature; United States and Canada, nd, American Library Association

Smith, Margarita Griggs, The San Simeon Story, (1958), Star-Reporter Publishing Company, San Luis Obispo

South County Historical Society, Yesterday, Today and Tomorrow; Volumes 1 through 5, various dates 1976-1989, South County

Historical Society, Arroyo Grande

Southern Pacific Railroad, List of Officers, Agencies and Stations, issued annually, dates reviewed 1887, 1894, 1899, 1904, 1918, Southern Pacific Railroad, NP

Southern Pacific Company, Coast Division Timetable 168, June 12, 1955, Southern Pacific Company, NP

Sperry, Baxter, Recollections of Eloisa Del Castillo Sifers, 1974, Laurel Hill Press, Galt, California

Squibb, Paul, Captain Portola in San Luis Obispo County in 1769, 1984, Tabula Rasa Press, San Luis Obispo

Stanley, Leo L., San Miguel at the Turn of the Century. 1976, Valley Publishers, Fresno

Stechman, John V., An Illustrated History of Land Acquisition and Development for Agricultural Education; California Polytechnic State University, 1985, California State Polytechnic University Foundation and John Stechman, San Luis Obispo

Stewart, George R., Names on the Land, 1945, Random House, New York

Stob, Ron, Back Roads of the Central Coast, 1986, Bear Flag Books, San Luis Obispo

Stob, Ron, More Back Roads of the Central Coast, 1989, Bear Flag Books, Arroyo Grande

Strother, Newell, *Lopez History*, unpublished ms., as quoted in *Place Names at Lopez Canyon*, by Elliot Curry, in La Vista, Volume 3, Number 4, January 1974, San Luis Obispo County Historical Society, San Luis Obispo

Strother, Newell, *Pioneers of Lopez Canyon*, in *La Vista*, Special Conference Edition, February, 1975, San Luis Obispo County Historical Society, San Luis Obispo

Thomason, Donalee Ludeke, Cholama the Beautiful One; Cholame Valley History and Its Pioneer People, 1988, Tabula Rasa Press, San Luis Obispo

Twisselmann, Ernest C., Flora of the Temblor Range, Fall, 1956, Wasmann Journal of Biology, University of San Francisco, San

Francisco

Van Harreveld, Constance, *Adobe Diary*, in *La Vista*, Special Conference Edition, February, 1975, San Luis Obispo County Historical Society, San Luis Obispo

Waltz, Marcus, Chronicles of Cambria's Pioneers, 1946, Marcus Waltz, Cambria

Watson, E.B., and Smith, Albert, Soil Survey of the Santa Maria Area, California, 1919, Government Printing Office, Washington

Weber, Msgr. Francis J., El Caminito Real; A Documentary History of California's Asistencias, 1988, Yee Ting Tong Printing Press Company, Hong Kong

Wells, Harry L., California Names, 1938, Kellaway-Ide Company, Los Angeles

Wheeler, Wendell, *Baywood Park, A Developers Gamble*, from *La Vista*, Volume 3, Number 2, January 1973, San Luis Obispo County Historical Society, San Luis Obispo

ORAL HISTORIES:

Adams, Mrs. Frank (Ella), Oral history interview, November 1, 1965, conducted by Mrs. Homer Waddoms and Louisiana Clayton Dart for the San Luis Obispo County Historical Society, transcript in the collection of the San Luis Obispo County Historical Museum

Adams, Mrs. Frank (Ella), KPRL "Pioneer Memories" interviews conducted by Phil Dirkx, nd, transcript provided by the Paso Robles Historical Society and on deposit at the San Luis Obispo County Historical Museum, SLO-KP-31 and SLO-KP-49

Ahrendt, William, Oral History interview, March 25, 1964, conducted for the San Luis Obispo County Historical Society, transcript in the collection of the San Luis Obispo County Historical Museum

Bethel, Edith, KPRL "Pioneer Memories" interview with Phil Dirkx, transcript provided by the Paso Robles Historical Society and on deposit at the San Luis Obispo County Historical Museum, SLO-KP-52

Davies, Lila, KPRL "Pioneer Memories" interviews conducted by Phil Dirkx, transcription done by the Paso Robles Historical Society on deposit at the San Luis Obispo County Historical Museum, SLO-KP-14, SLO-KP-18

Dayton, Velma and Clyde, Oral History Interview, May 15, 1965, conducted by Mrs. Marian _____ (name is not transcribed) with Mrs. Emma McChesney and Mrs. Homer L. Odom for the of the San Luis Obispo County Historical Society, transcript in the collection of the San Luis Obispo County Historical Museum

Klintworth, Henry, Oral History Interview, September 25, 1969, conducted by Homer Wadhams for the San Luis Obispo County Historical Society, transcription provided by the Paso Robles Historical Society, transcript and original on deposit at the San Luis Obispo County Historical Museum, SLO-HS-97

Machado, Bill, Oral History, September 18, 1978, Conducted by Dan and Liz Krieger for the San Luis Obispo County Historical Society, transcript on deposit at the San Luis Obispo County Historical Museum, SLO-HS-74

O'Donovan, Ambrose, Oral History done for the San Luis Obispo County Historical Society, Conducted by Mrs. Wadhams, transcript provided by the Paso Robles Historical Society and on deposit, with original tape recording, at the San Luis Obispo County Historical Museum, SLO-HS-48

Quinn, Jack, KPRL "Pioneer Memories" interview conducted by Phil Dirkx, transcript provided by the Paso Robles Historical Society and on deposit at the San Luis Obispo County Historical Society, SLO-KP-2

Renaud, Maud and Cruess, Ruth, Oral history done for the Friends of the Adobes with Ray Harden, April 1972, transcription done by the Paso Robles Historical Society on deposit at the San Luis Obispo County Historical Society, SLO-FA-01

Stanley, Dr. Leo, KPRL "Pioneer Memory" interview conducted by Phil Dirkx, transcript provided by Paso Robles Historical Society and on deposit at the San Luis Obispo County Historical Society, SLO-KP-8

Thorndyke, Loren and Maude, Oral History, August 5, 1965, Conducted by Paul Squibb for the San Luis Obispo County Historical Society, transcript on deposit at the San Luis Obispo County

Historical Museum, SLO-HS-30

Truesdale, Willis and Zora, Oral History, April 1, 1964, Conducted by Gertrude Truesdale Hailey for the San Luis Obispo County Historical Society, transcript in the Collection of the San Luis Obispo County Historical Museum, SLO-HS-9

Tyson, Frank, Oral History, February 3, 1966, Conducted by Mrs. Homer Wadhams, Mr. and Mrs. Paul Squibb and Mr. Emma McChesney, for the San Luis Obispo County Historical Society, transcript in the Collection of the San Luis Obispo County Historical Museum, SLO-HS-37

White, George, Oral History, date not recorded, Conducted by Lillian Wadhams for the San Luis Obispo County Historical Society, transcript on deposit at the San Luis Obispo County Historical Museum, SLO-HS-21

MAPS:

Coast and Geodetic Survey, coastal topographic maps, Estero Bay (1940), Point Conception to Point Sur (1941), Point Dume to Purisima Point (1940), San Luis Obispo Bay/Port San Luis (1938)

County of San Luis Obispo, Official Map of the County, 1874, 1890, 1941

United States Geologic Service, Quadrangle Maps, Adelaida (1948 and 15 min. 1961), Arroyo Grande 15 min. (1925 and 1965), Atascadero 7.5 min. (1965), Branch Mountain 7.5 min. (1967), Caldwell Mesa 7.5 min. (1967), Caliente Mountain 15 min. (1959), California Valley 7.5 min. (1966), Camatta Canyon 7.5 min. (1976), Camatta Ranch 7.5 min. (1966), Cambria 7.5 min. (1979), Cayucos (1943), Chimney Canyon 7.5 min. (1967), Cholame 7.5 min (1961), Cholame Hills 7.5 min. (1976, Cholame Valley 7.5 min. (1961, Creston 7.5 min. (1980), Cypress Mountain 7.5 min. (1979), La Panza 15 min. (1952), La Panza 7.5 min. (1967), La Panza NE 7.5 min. (1973, La Panza Ranch 7.5 min. (1966, Las Yeguas 7.5 min. (1959). Lime Mountain (1948), Lopez 15 min. (1965), Maricopa (1951), Nipomo 7.5 min. (1965), Oceano 7.5 min. (1979), Orchard Peak 15 min. (1961), Panorama Hills (1954), Port San Luis (1951), Pozo 15 min. (1952), Ranchito Canyon (1948), Reward (1951), San Luis Obispo (1965), San Simeon (1958), Templeton (1948), Wells Ranch (1954), York Mountain (1948)

Key to the USGS Map Quadrangles

C5	Adelaida	H11	Miranda Pine Mountain
G7	Arroyo Grande NE	E5	Morro Bay North
E6	Atascadero	F5	Morro Bay South
I16	Ballinger Canyon	I14	New Cuyama
I12	Bates Canyon	H8	Nipomo
B5	Bradley	H7	Oceano
G11	Branch Mountain	C10	Orchard Peak
B3	Bryson	D11	Packwood Creek
B2	Burnett Peak	G13	Painted Rock
B1	Burro Mountain	G14	Panorama Hills
G9	Caldwell Mesa	C6	Paso Robles
H13	Caliente Mountain	I13	Peak Mountain
F11	California Valley	C3	Pebblestone Shut-in
D9	Camatta Canyon	D2	Pico Creek
E9	Camatta Ranch	C1	Piedras Blancas
D3	Cambria	G6	Pismo Beach
E4	Cayucos	I6	Point Sal
G12	Chimineas Ranch	G5	Port San Luis
H10	Chimney Canyon	F9	Pozo Summit
C9	Cholame	B7	Ranchito Canyon
B8	Cholame Hills	F14	Reward
B9	Cholame Valley	F6	San Luis Obispo
D7	Creston	B6	San Miguel
I15	Cuyama	C2	San Simeon
D4	Cypress Mountain	E7	Santa Margarita
H15	Elkhorn Hills	F8	Santa Margarita Lake
C7	Estrella	I8	Santa Maria
I7	Guadalupe	C8	Shandon
D10	Holland Canyon	D8	Shedd Canyon
H9	Huasna Peak	F12	Simmler
F10	La Panza	G8	Tar Spring Ridge
E11	La Panza NE	H12	Taylor Canyon
E10	La Panza Ranch	D6	Templeton
E12	Las Yuegas Ranch	B10	Tent Hills
C4	Lime Mountain	I10	Tepusquet Canyon
F7	Lopez Mountain	B4	Tierra Redonda Mtn.
G10	Los Machos Hills	I9	Twitchell Dam
I11	Manzanita Mountain	H14	Wells Ranch
H16	Maricopa	E8	Wilson Corner
F13	Mc Kittrick Summit	D5	York Mountain